Sacred Companions
Sacred Community

✦

Reflections with Clare of Assisi

Megan Don

Author of Falling Into the Arms of God

iUniverse, Inc.

New York Bloomington Shanghai

Sacred Companions Sacred Community
Reflections with Clare of Assisi

iUniverse books may be ordered through booksellers or by contacting:

iUniverse
1663 Liberty Drive
Bloomington, IN 47403
www.iuniverse.com
1-800-Authors (1-800-288-4677)

Because of the dynamic nature of the Internet, any Web addresses or links contained in this book may have changed since publication and may no longer be valid.

The views expressed in this work are solely those of the author and do not necessarily reflect the views of the publisher, and the publisher hereby disclaims any responsibility for them.

ISBN: 978-0-595-47068-6 (pbk)
ISBN: 978-0-595-91350-3 (ebk)

Printed in the United States of America

My journey with Clare of Assisi has been one of sitting at the feet of a masterful soul skilled in the way of compassion and tender love. Her generosity and gentleness never fail to bring me into a place of depth and breadth that far exceeds the human comprehension of what it means to love. I am deeply grateful for her teachings, and her quiet, yet strong presence in my life. I hope that through these writings you will come to know her wisdom, allow your soul to be transformed, and bring your own self love into the world.

To love deeply in one direction makes us more loving in all others.

—Anne-Sophie Swetchine

Contents

TOUCH: THE ORIGINAL EMBRACE

FULLNESS OF THE SENSES: MYSTICAL UNION

FOREWORD

Clare has always been overshadowed by her partner, Francis. Culture, until very recently, has tended to see women largely as appendages to the men in their lives. Most of our mothers signed their name "Mrs. John Smith", and thought nothing of it. I am sure Clare herself, so perfectly free of herself, was quite content to be merely known as Francis' sidekick.

But *we* can no longer be content, nor would Francis be content with such an arrangement, nor will history be content. We know too much now—about her, about her parallel identity and complementary spirituality, and about how we all suffer when the feminine side, and her side in this case, is overlooked, subsumed, or even denied.

We friars always saw that Francis was a bit of a fanatic in regard to poverty, and then sent us toward an extroverted, career-oriented lifestyle that largely made it impossible or at least highly impractical. His radical poverty was forgotten almost immediately by most of his male followers. It was only Clare who created a lifestyle where it could actually be lived.

Francis also lived and taught a radical humility, yet he sent us into a public, status conscious, and clerical domain where humility was neither admired nor sought after. We ended up paying lip service to humility, but by reason of accepting priesthood and leadership roles, often found ourselves no more humble than other priests, prelates, or professionals. Layfolks usually put us to shame here. Clare, however, created a situation of "structural humility"—where you could not fake it but had to face your own inner nothingness day by day. There was no one to impress except God alone.

Francis, of course, was primarily working with men. After living in various male Franciscan communities since the late 1950's, working with male spirituality since the mid 1980's, and giving retreats to monasteries and male congregations throughout the world, I do know that celibate males do not naturally or readily live in community. Spiritual and intimate conversation does not come easily to us, and in fact, we somewhat aggressively avoid it. Many male friaries and monasteries are more akin to friendly hotels than hothouses of spirituality. I think most of my confreres would sadly agree with me on that.

We have often admired our Poor Clare sisters from a distance because we knew they had honest community, spiritual conversation, a contemplative prayer style, plus a radical humility and poverty that we could only dream about. We knew that we had become workers in a very busy and often frenetic culture and church. At our worst, we were diocesan priests in brown habits; at our best (which happens with some regularity) we did church very differently than a lot of clergy. Gospel came first, and "churchianity" was second. The peoples' needs came first, and then the hierarchy's. Francis and Clare both taught us to put Jesus out in front, and to see the church as a vehicle for that vision. We sadly recognized that the vehicle often takes over the road, and that it is hard to criticize the very vehicle that is giving you your status, your identity, and your social security. The Poor Clares avoided that, and Clare taught them how. She was right to speak of her rule as the "privilege of poverty."

Just as Clare was overlooked in favor of Francis, I think Clare's virtues and spirituality were often overlooked in favor of what I call "birdbath Franciscanism". More sentiment than radical Gospel, pious but not any kind of revolution, more riding on the coat tails of a universally admired image than living the lifestyle ourselves. Without Clare's Gospel radicalism, grounded in contemplation, I suppose this was inevitable. Nobody's fault, no bad will, nothing against men (I am one myself!), but just what happens when you have too much outside and not enough inside, too much busyness and not enough groundedness, roles and functions instead of prayer, too much male bravado and performance without much intimate presence and silence.

But in this book by Megan Don you are going to hear about some of those wonderful and much needed "Clarissan" values. A book like this can—and will—move you beyond any "birdbath Franciscanism" into a spirituality that is for women and men, for celibates and part-nered, for extroverts and introverts, for people with souls and bodies, and even people both Christian and non Christian.

If you will allow me to play out my metaphor, this kind of wisdom will help you take flight out of the birdbath and into the open skies of the Spirit.

Fr. Richard Rohr, O.F.M.
Center for Action and Contemplation
Albuquerque, New Mexico

INTRODUCTION

A saint is one who exaggerates what the world neglects.

—G.K. Chesterton

Our world today is filled with souls who are searching for love. This search, this seeking, is now emerging as a longing for a love of deeper and broader dimensions than we have so far known or lived. Our desire is to know intimately the love that created us, and the love that daily sustains us. We look in many places for this love, and most seek it in a special companion. But again, our innate longing is for a new and more soulful companionship, one that is founded in spirit and the greater love of God. It is now the age of breaking down the old frameworks of projected romanticism and psychological battle, and a time of bringing forward the possibilities of a renewed relating, with our own souls, with others, and with God.

We all ultimately seek our own self-love, and it is through journeying with our companions and our community, with consciousness and deep awareness, that we can find this most treasured place within. The emotional evolution of the human soul has dictated, and is still dictating, the ways in which our relationships are formed and lived. As we have experienced, and witnessed, this relating can create havoc in our lives and souls if undertaken from a psychological basis alone. We have forgotten that the very foundation of love is in our spiritual nature. This greater essence of love is the container in which all of our emotional and physical needs are held. If they are not held and nourished here, we run amok, chasing one desire after another, one person after another, seeking fulfillment in places that can never satisfy our need of sacred love. We are now invited to partake in this fulfillment.

The saints have much to teach us about the sacredness of love, and in particular, the life of the thirteenth-century saint, Clare of Assisi provides an illuminated pathway. Her life is a great example of a journey into self-love through her intimate relationship with her spiritual companion, Francis of Assisi. Clare's journey, though, was not an easy one; it required much death to the continual perceptions and desires of the ego self. By it, however, she entered into the truth of a greater love, which ultimately fed her, as a woman, as a teacher and spiritual counselor, and as the leader of a new spiritual community. It is her journey that inspires this work, and as we walk with Clare, we will come to understand the fears that stop us from loving, the constructs of the mind that are always trying to keep the unknown at bay, and the depth of love that is begging us to look within and to accept this love as our own.

This work also seeks to return us to the sacredness of the body, and the role of the sacred in our intimate relating and lovemaking. Here we deviate from the lives of the saints or, perhaps, expand upon their lives, through using the spiritual foundation as the basis for bodily intimacy. This is something the Eastern countries and religions have known for many centuries. In the West, unfortunately, this knowledge has been denied, buried, and burned. It is now up to us to reclaim the truth of our bodies, to experience them as vessels for enlightening the soul, and to know that our image is truly that of God. The meditations throughout this book are devised to introduce and enhance this age-old wisdom.

As we walk on this earth, we will encounter many sacred companions. Discernment and maturity of spirit are needed in order to understand what kind of companionship we are to have with each of them. Often our behavior can be rashly based on cherished desires rather than on the reality of the situation and the person before us. Throughout this book we will be challenged to look again and again at our unconscious motives, reaching into the depths of our self, and coming into clarity and the true nature of what we are living.

ABOUT CLARE OF ASSISI:

She shone forth in life; she is radiant after death.

—*The Lady*, 264

Clare was born in Assisi, Italy, c. 1193–94 to noble parentage. Her mother, Ortulana, was firmly grounded in her religious beliefs, as well as given to an independence rare for her time. She traveled on pilgrimages, with women companions only, and created something akin to a women's lay community in her home, with the emphasis on prayer and almsgiving. Drawing close to the time of giving birth to her first child, she undertook a rigorous pilgrimage to the shrine of St. Michael in Mount Gargano, Italy. At the shrine, she heard these words: "You will give birth to a light that will shine brilliantly in the world." Taking the prophecy seriously, Ortulana named her child Chiara, or Clare, meaning "light."

Clare's father, Favarone, like many nobility of his time, was a knight who was often away from home, waging war with encroaching outsiders or participating in the next ordered crusade. The romanticism of knighthood is a grave misconception; the reality was much bloodshed and loss of life. This was the other influence alive in Clare's household: seven burly knights in the form of brothers and uncles. She was later to experience their warring tactics aimed at her rather than protecting her.

Clare's life of listening to God began at a young age. She was following the example of prayer and almsgiving set by the women in her home; however she quickly learned to find her own way of living out these values. Not satisfied with giving mere surplus to the poor, she gave of her own food. As was the custom of the day for noblewomen, Clare received a large inheritance of property. There was an understanding that it was to be joined with her future husband's fortune as a dowry. But Clare had other ideas. She sold off this inheritance and gave all the money to the poor. At that time, she dedicated her life to God. She was not yet eighteen.

Clare was definitely paving a new life; even her women companions were shocked at this seemingly perilous undertaking. How was she to survive? "Through the grace of God," came Clare's reply. And no amount of wooing or promised riches from noble suitors could change her mind. The first signs of absolute commitment to her chosen life were clearly displayed.

Francis of Assisi has, unfortunately, overshadowed Clare's luminous life; most people do not even know of her existence, nor do they know that Clare and Francis were intimate spiritual companions. It is unknown exactly when they met—we can estimate that it was around 1210, when Clare was sixteen. It is assumed that Clare heard Francis preach after his conversion experience (he was previously a great enjoyer of wine, women, and song) and then began to follow him. Clare's youngest sister, Beatrice, however, reports otherwise: that Francis heard of Clare's holiness and sought to visit her. This was the beginning of many visitations over the next two years.

Fearful of her family's repudiation—Francis did not have a good reputation, even as a religious his sanity was questioned—Clare often left her home and secretly visited Francis. Their relationship was developing, and it was clear to both that their desire to live the gospel by becoming "poor in spirit" and relying solely on the love of God was the divine thread that was binding them. This spiritual basis was also giving birth to a love of grander dimensions between them, that of woman and man. The mirror of love was being held for both to see their divine reflections in each other. Both fell deeply into this pool of love.

On Palm Sunday, 1212, Clare boldly left the security of her family home to join Francis and his itinerant brothers. Francis received her into his way of life, and Clare stepped into that initiation with no knowledge of what the night, let alone the rest of her still young life, would bring. She had desires and plans, of course: to be with Francis and the brothers, feeding the poor and the lepers, and living the love that burned so fiercely in her soul. She felt great freedom in leaving the expectations of her family and noble society; and being a great lover of nature, she was looking forward to roaming the hills of Assisi with Francis.

This initial euphoria, unfortunately, was short-lived. Francis, confused about how to live with Clare and fearing for her reputation and safety, arranged for her to be temporarily housed with a nearby Benedictine community. He then moved her to another church before taking her to San Damiano, which was to be her home for the rest of her life. Why did Francis invite Clare to join him and initiate her into his brothers' way of life if he was going to distance her like this? I personally believe that Francis feared the great love between him and Clare. His bodily passions were a constant struggle for him, and I believe he simply did not know how to enter into this love with the fullness that it required.

This perspective begs the question, Why did Francis choose to be celibate? He was not a priest, and therefore celibacy was not required of him. Celibacy, however, had been a prevalent issue since the end of the eleventh-century. The law of celibacy for priests was being instituted, and celibacy was being professed as spiritually more "pure" than marriage and sexual relations. We must also remember Francis's earlier life, in which he had not respected his sexuality and the significance of sexual relations. In the light of the Church teaching, his spiritual conversion, and his previous personal behavior, I think the pendulum for Francis swung to the extreme of abstinence.

And what of Clare's desires? I think she was willing to love him no matter what form their love took. This willingness caused her the greatest pain, and the greatest joy. She and Francis both endured the joy and pain of the purging fire through their love for each another. Or as Auspicious Van Constanje, O.F.M., writes, "They discovered in each other the same luxury of God's presence and the same fire that consumed all the idols of their hearts, until they were ash."

Their destinies were clearly bound together. Francis rebuilt the San Damiano church through divine direction. He prophesied that "holy ladies" would inhabit this place even before Clare joined him. The air of serenity and sweet love still pervades this church today, and you can feel the soul of Clare as you pray in the chapel and walk in the olive groves. If you listen carefully, you can even hear the purity of her voice echoing in the choir stalls. Francis needed Clare to help balance his intensity. She provided a feminine love and energy of tender strength. Clare needed Francis to help balance her austerity. He provided a masculine reason and insight that she could not contact for herself. They provided for each other as soul companions.

Clare left us a minimal but rich resource, in the form of her writings: four letters to Agnes of Prague that demonstrate the depth of her spiritual love and understanding; *The Testament*, in which she writes about the building of the community through "vocation and choice"; *The Rule*, or *Form of Life*, as she preferred to call it, which gives clear guidelines for community life but with versatility and adaptability; and *The Blessing*, Clare's last words to her sisters, with a reminder to "always be lovers of your souls." There are also a small number of works written about Clare or where she is mentioned.

In this book, I draw primarily on Clare's letters to Agnes of Prague, which use the framework of the senses to describe her great communion with love, at once mystical yet deeply grounded in this world. The six parts of the book address the five senses and add what I call "the fullness of the senses" or mystical union, which tells of the deepening connection between Clare and Francis throughout their lives.

Clare was the first woman in the Church to write, and have officially accepted, a rule for a community of women. It took much patience for this accomplishment to be realized. The great turnover of Popes during her lifetime did not help her situation. And even though some Popes were supportive and recognized her acclaimed sanctity, they still interjected their own or other existing rules, all written by men. Nevertheless, Clare held steadfast, and on August 9, 1253, she received the Papal Bull of approval from Innocent IV. She was sixty years old. Her mission for establishing community was finally and officially complete. Two days later, on August 11, she passed on to her next life. On August 15, 1255, Clare was canonized a saint by Pope Alexander IV.

Clare's intimate relationships with God and her own soul were of paramount importance to her; then came Francis, and her community life. All were inextricably bound by love and flowed in and through one another, but ultimately, Clare knew that nothing was possible without the grace of God. This was her foundation, from which all else in her life developed.

May Clare's life illuminate your heart as you seek your own love, the love of God and companion, and the creation of a loving community. May we all learn from her wisdom, and her simple message of love and compassion, and know that we too can live in this way, bringing the manifestation of love into a lived reality in our world. As Ann Johnson has written in *Miryam of Jerusalem*, "God creates each one of us as endless community." Now is the time of sacred companions and sacred community.

HOW TO READ THIS BOOK

FOR INDIVIDUAL READERS

This book may be read in two ways. The first is sequentially: by reading chapters consecutively, you will be taken on a journey that deepens your experience of the sacredness of relating. Do not be in a hurry to move from one chapter to the next; your soul may wish to linger, and contemplate in depth, the lesson that is being offered. Let the spirit guide you.

The second way to read this book is through random selection. Sit quietly, coming into the stillness of your being, and ask to be given the reading that is most relevant for you in that moment. You may do this when your soul is feeling disturbed or simply as a morning or evening meditation.

Whichever way you choose to read the book, let your time with it be a time of entering into the sacredness of your own being. Let it be a time of communing with love. Make for yourself a special place where you will not be disturbed, and invite the Spirit of God and Clare to be with you. Breathe deeply into your soul, and spend a few moments in the quiet; free yourself from your regular daily activities and devote your whole attention to the reading. Familiarize yourself with the theme you are reading about—located at the beginning of each sense—then turn to the relevant chapter. Ask that you will be open to the blessing that awaits you.

Each chapter consists of a quotation from Clare's writing, some reflective words, and then two meditations. I suggest that you first read the quotation from Clare's writing, then the reflective words, allowing your own experiences, thoughts, and feelings to arise as you read. Then go back to the quotation and read the words slowly and deliberately, letting them penetrate deeply within. Finally turn to the meditation. Decide if you wish to do the meditation alone or with your companion. Most of the meditations may be entered into alone or with another, and are equally suitable for persons in a relationship or those who are single and journeying on their own.

Prepare yourself for actively entering the meditation. Seat yourself comfortably, slowly breathe in and breathe out, being aware of the breath moving through the whole of your body. Gently return to the meditation and follow its guidance. Throughout the meditation, allow the Spirit to guide you to the most relevant place for your soul. Complete your meditation with a prayer of gratitude.

Enjoy and be gentle with yourself!

FOR GROUP STUDY

This book is well suited to study and discussion groups. For use with others I suggest that each participant make a commitment to yourself, to God, and to the group for six weeks. You will work with one chapter from each of the six senses. Each week let a different member of the group choose the chapter. Begin with a short prayer, welcoming all the members and inviting the Spirit and Clare to be with you, and to guide you on your exploration. Come into silence, and through the breath, move into the stillness of your being (you may wish to spend a short time simply following the breath through inhalation and exhalation). When all are ready, the leader can slowly read the quotation from Clare at the beginning of the chosen chapter once and then again. Then the leader can read the reflection.

Once the reflection has been read, open the group for members to speak about thoughts and experiences that have arisen from the reading. Participants should keep their words brief and to the point—it is our minds that have much to say; our hearts can speak very concisely!

Honor each one's contribution without the need to fix or interpret. When all who wish to speak have spoken, lead the group back into the breath and silence.

Slowly repeat the quotation and lead the companion meditation, giving time and space for the words to penetrate the soul and the Spirit to guide the meditative experience. Do not be in a hurry. The leader will close the group when the time feels appropriate, with a blessing for all in the group, for all their companions, for the wider community, and for the world, giving gratitude for the blessings we always receive.

This above format is a recommendation only, and may be altered according to each group's need and inspiration.

FOR COMMUNITY STUDY

This book is also devised to enable the process of creating and renewing community—something in which Clare showed great expertise. Let each participant make a commitment to yourself, to God, and to the group for six weeks. You will work with one chapter from each of the six senses. You may designate a leader for the whole six-week study or let a different member of the community lead each week. Begin with a short prayer, welcoming all the community members and inviting the Spirit and Clare to be with you and to guide you on your exploration. Come into silence, and through the breath, move into the stillness of your being (you may wish to spend a short time simply following the breath through inhalation and exhalation). When all are ready, the leader can slowly read the quotation from Clare at the beginning of the chosen chapter once and then again. Then the leader can read the reflection. Slowly repeat the quotation and lead the community meditation, giving time and space for the words to penetrate the soul and for the Spirit to guide the meditative experience.

When it feels appropriate, the leader may open the group for members to speak about thoughts and experiences from the meditation and reading. Participants should keep their words brief and to the point—it is our minds that have much to say; our hearts can speak very concisely! Honor each one's contribution without the need to fix or interpret. When all who wish to speak have spoken, lead the group back into the breath and silence. Ask the Spirit to show how this experience may help form or re-form your community. Lay down your own will and say, "Thy will be done."

Close with a prayer of gratitude for your own soul, for your companions in your group and church community, for all the souls in your wider community and in the world. Ask that they may all be blessed with love.

This format is a recommendation only, and may be altered according to each community's need and inspiration.

I gathered the quotations principally from two sources, and from this point on, I indicate these sources using the following abbreviations: **Early Docs.,** for *Clare of Assisi, Early Documents,* and **The Lady,** for *Clare of Assisi, The Lady, Early Documents.* In some cases the quotations are taken from other sources, which will be indicated and found in the bibliography under Resources at the back of the book. Unless otherwise indicated all biblical quotes are from the New King James Version of the bible. Where NJ is written, these quotes are taken from the New Jerusalem Bible. All Rumi quotes are taken from *Open Secret: Versions of Rumi,* translated by John Moyne and Coleman Barks.

Sight: The Lover's Gaze

No, Love does not abandon us;
we ourselves turn our faces
from the Light.

—Nan C. Merrill, Psalm 44

Our inner mystical vision and our outer physical sight are two blessed gifts from God. As we traverse this earth on our spiritual evolutionary journey, we often turn aside from these gifts, either denying them or simply not being conscious of them. Either way, God is calling us back to take full possession of what is rightfully ours.

In this sense Clare invites us into the consciousness of our being and teaches us the art of contemplation, that is, seeing the eternal. We are reminded how important sight is in our sacred relating and in being able to see the "holiness" of ourselves and another. Clare holds up the divine mirror of the Christ consciousness and asks us to look deep within. She tells us not to be afraid to gaze fully upon our own beauty.

1

Before The Beginning

When she began to feel the first stirrings of holy love, she judged that the passing scene of worldly pride should be condemned, being taught by the unction of the Spirit to place a worthless price upon worthless things.

—***The Lady***, 282

As we enter into a maturity of being, our awareness of how we wish to live becomes more acute. We have learnt from past experience things we do not wish to repeat and situations we choose not to entertain. There is wisdom in foreseeing an entanglement that is not desirable for the soul's growth, and even greater wisdom in following this understanding. Clare, at a young age, had a "holy knowing" of how she wished to live her life and a definite resolve about what she did not want to do.

She reminds us in the Second Letter to Agnes (*Early Docs*, 40), to "always remember your resolution and be conscious of your beginning." How often do we decide on a new way of behavior and then, while the resolve is still fresh upon our lips, find ourselves once more living that same old pattern? Remember your resolution and walk away. Be conscious of your beginning; that is, return to your purity of thought, word, and action. Return to the very sacredness of your being. How easily we fall into our lower nature, and yet this nature is a mere shadow of our spiritual potential, and it provides only temporary satisfaction.

3

Clare writes that we must offer ourselves as a "pleasing sacrifice" (*Early Docs*, 40) to the divine love. The word sacrifice conveys a distinctly negative connotation to our contemporary minds, and can alienate us from further inquiry. Robert Johnson, in *Balancing Heaven and Earth*, however, provides a definition that opens this word and world to us. He writes that "sacrifice is an act of transformation where energy is taken from a lower plane of existence and transformed into a higher place of thought and action." It is, if you like, an alchemical transmutation. It is not "going without" or "giving up something" but rather bringing that action into its purest possible expression.

Clare sacrificed the world of pride, acquisition, and arranged marriage for a life devoted to realizing her soul potential and consciousness. Her acute inner vision was not forsaken for outer appearances or desires, and she certainly did not feel she was missing out on life. She was entering the truth of her soul and the sacredness of living. This crucial decision occurred before Clare's meeting with Francis; otherwise their souls would not have met as equals. She could easily have fallen into an unhealthy reliance, projecting her innate soul desires onto Francis rather than claiming and living them in and for herself.

So too we must resolve to live in the fullness of the light of our consciousness, ever moving towards our infinite potential. We must be willing to sacrifice, that is, to transform our lower natures and desires and once more return to, and live from, our inner purity. In this way we will come into connection again and again with our soul mates, both intimately and in community.

Companion Meditation:
Come into a place of quiet, both externally and internally, allowing the rhythm of the breath to calm and soothe your soul. Let yourself gently move through the layers of mind and soul, connecting with the purity of your Spirit. See how you may rely on your companion, or another, in an unhealthy way. See where you may have denied your original purity. Let

the Spirit show you how to gently come back into the truth of your own
being. Give thanks to both Spirit and companion.

Community Meditation:
Gathering together in respect and openness, let the Spirit guide you into
the quietness of being. See how the community is devoted to the light of
consciousness being reflected in every member. See where you individually
may fall into your lower nature of response. Allow the spirit of the community to raise you and bind you back to your own purity, supporting
and guiding where necessary. Allow your world of pride to dissolve into
the loving arms of your spirit companions.

2

The First Glance

Happy, indeed, is she ...
... Whose remembrance delightfully dawns

—The Lady, 54–55

This human living is a mysterious journey. Different parts of our nature are revealed, sometimes with slow and subtle tones and at other times with great immediacy and intensity. There is no rule as to how or what we will experience, or when. It seems to me that the Spirit delights in constantly surprising us with Her gifts of love, whether we think we are ready or not!

One area of our life where this mystery is evident is in our meetings with others. Here we can experience an immediate connection with another merely through that first glance, the first resting of the eyes upon each other. Worlds can open, and there can be a sense of knowing this person, a remembering if you like, or a dawning of a known light within. Psalm 112:4 tells us, "Light dawns for the gracious and compassionate." And this is what is experienced in this meeting, a sense of compassion for the other and a gracious understanding of her or his soul. Somehow the two souls are already in the depths of communing, and the physical meeting is now bringing this into consciousness. As the Sufi poet Rumi writes,

"Lovers don't finally meet somewhere.
They're in each other all along" (19).

The body also experiences a quickening with such a meeting, as if all the cells are suddenly being awoken. There is a feeling of aliveness similar to that of "falling in love." And, of course, that is what is happening; an innate love is being reborn.

What is required of us is the ability to discern when these connections are to develop into something more intimate and when they are to remain as soul friends only. Often we mistakenly throw ourselves into the ocean of intimate love and end up battered by the waves. Our contemporary world is permeated with hurriedness, and our approach to love is no exception. Discernment requires that we allow these connections to unfold without wanting to make them anything other than two souls meeting. The true nature of the love will be revealed as we continue living our lives with an innocence of being, that is, without plans and manipulations.

When Clare met Francis, did she have an immediate knowing of his soul? I think she did. If not, she would not have met him in secret on several occasions. By meeting Francis secretly, she was jeopardizing her highly esteemed "virginal honor," and thus her whole future. Clearly the connection between Clare and Francis was known instantly to both, which prompted them to further their exploration into each other's souls. Love was calling them from on high, and they were both courageous enough to answer, letting this very spirit of love lead them. May we, like Clare and Francis, follow the spirit of love when it calls us, allowing discernment to show us the true nature of its being.

Companion Meditation:
Settle quietly into your being. Allow memories of your first meeting with your companion to arise. Was there an instant connection? What conceptions did you have at that time? Did you plan and manipulate, or did you allow the spirit of love to unfold? Hold all of this in love, and ask that your love be blessed with purity, washing clean any old behaviors. Let the Spirit renew your love.

Community Meditation:
Gathering in the quietness, join together with the intent of entering deeply into the community spirit of love. Allow memories to arise of meetings with others in your community. Notice any feelings of love, and let them expand in your heart. See any judgments, and ask that they be washed clean. Let yourself drown in the spirit of community love.

3

Holy Sight

Happy, indeed, is she ...
... Whose glorious vision will bless.

—Early Docs., 48

The gift of sight is a blessing. We absorb so much of our world by our vision, and we can also give so much in return through a momentary glance. The sheer wonder of this body is also revealed in the interrelationship between the eyes, the mind, and the heart. There is a constant communication among these faculties, informing our opinions, our lessons, our pleasures and pains.

Andreas Capellanus wrote in his twelth-century medieval treatise on love, "For when a man sees some woman fit for love ... he begins at once to lust after her in his heart; then the more he thinks about her, the more he burns with love, until he comes to a fuller meditation" (Camille, 29). Here we witness the intricate interrelationship between sight, thought, and feeling. But in addition we are told of a deeper internal space that the smitten lover is brought into. The attraction is not immediately acted on, but a "fuller meditation" is entered into. In this way the one who is stirring the heart is not pursued as an object of possession but is taken into the sacred place of the heart. The eyes now look from this inner sanctuary and not from the initial place of lust or gain. This shift, by the way, is equally relevant for both male and female.

9

How do we feel when we are looked upon with lustful desire? If we are also entertaining such thoughts, perhaps the attraction will eventuate into a temporary bodily pleasure. But if we have taken a step into our mature being and are living from a "fuller meditation," then only an equally deep response will satisfy. A look of real love, a silent yet active communication of compassion and vision, penetrates the heart and blesses the soul. This is the holy sight—compassion for the human self that we are now, and vision for the divine self that wants to be revealed. With this fullness of sight, the whole self, including the body, is loved in an instant.

This holy sight was a gift of Clare's. She was able to bless all through her vision because she had clearly entered into the wisdom of the Beatitudes, that is, "Blessed are the pure in heart, for they shall see God" (Matt. 5:8). Clare was known to easily excuse those around her for what she called their "human frailties." Offensive behaviors did not cause Clare to love any less. Her gaze remained constant in love, and she saw only the purity of those before her. She wrote that God did not see any imperfection in us, and that we must learn to see with these same eyes. What a blessing to not see what we consider to be imperfections, both in ourselves and in others!

Herein lies the wisdom of Clare; a human frailty or weakness is not an imperfection, it is merely the lower nature, which can be transformed in the twinkling of an eye, or through a blessed glance of love. As it is written in Proverbs 15:30 (NJ), *A kindly glance gives joy to the heart.* What will it take for our human psyches to relinquish our self-condemnation and truly love ourselves? Perhaps one way is to look to Clare's life and, like her, rely totally on the Spirit to accomplish everything. We can bring ourselves into the divine presence and allow God's gaze to rest upon us. We can let it penetrate into our deepest hearts, and let it wash clean our mind and thoughts, ridding us of our self-hatred. Only then can we gaze upon another with the holy sight of love.

Companion Meditation:
Bring yourself into the quiet of your being. Ask the Spirit to reveal to you anything that you may consider an imperfection about yourself—then let the gaze of God rest upon you, all of you. Feel the all-encompassing love. Now consider any perceived imperfections in your companion—let God gaze through your eyes and soul upon your companion. See the beauty of who you both are and how you are both evolving into your God-selves.

Community Meditation:
Come together with the intent of questioning how your community gazes upon itself and upon the world. Bring yourselves into the silence of God and let the Spirit lead you into your own gaze. Are you seeing through the holy sight as you look upon your community? If there is a block, allow the Spirit to direct you. Then let your gaze broaden to the world. With what sight do you view the world? Let God bless you and gaze through you.

4

The Mirror of Truth

Gaze upon that mirror each day,
and continually study your face in it,
that you may adorn yourself completely,
within and without.

—*The Lady*, 55

The mirror was a potent symbol of the medieval era. Though there can be no one meaning ascribed to it, we witness its use by poets, religious, and artisans to portray an aspect of love. One poet likens his beloved to a "mirror, clear, shining, unsullied," in which he could see himself and also the love of his lady. The famous set of tapestries, *The Lady with the Unicorn*, uses the mirror as a major symbol, as does a medallion, *The Virgin Traps the Unicorn*, created nearly two hundred years earlier (Camille, 47).

The mirror also held special significance for Clare, and she used it frequently in her gentle way of teaching. In the quotation for this chapter, it is the mirror of the Christ image that she speaks of. We are to come and gaze upon the Christ gazing at us. What a powerful image. We will encounter not only the truthfulness of our own reflection but also "the radiance of eternal glory" (*The Lady*, 55). In this way, if we see any hypocrisy, any bitterness, anger, or other unpleasant truths within ourselves, they are met by the elevating consciousness of the Christ source. The reflection of truth does not need to be an experience of further self-hatred, it can be evolving and healing. Clare writes, "Place your mind before the mirror of eternity!" (*The Lady*, 51). Understanding the mind and its propensity to complicate and create false notions, Clare tells us to place our mind before this mirror. Let it also enjoy the radiance of the Christ being, allowing for an "adornment" both within and without. That is, the eternal source of our inner nature will bring the mind into a peaceful and loving place, and this orientation will be reflected in our outer nature or actions. As we love within, so we shall love without.

God provides us with many mirrors in our lives. Unknown people we meet during the course of a day, the child playing in the park, our colleagues, and very often, with greater intensity, our intimate companions and community. Once we bring awareness into this continual reflective process, it no longer falls prey to projection. Irritations and annoyances are no longer thrown back at the other person in the form of judgment; they are seen for what they are—aspects of ourselves that are not loved. Take the time to love yourself back into the radiance, and remember, there are no imperfections!

Similarly, when we are attracted to aspects within another, we are simply seeing the radiant part of our own nature. Because we have not been taught how to recognize and claim the love we have for our own self, we also project this onto the other. And then we claim it is they, not we, who are adorned with such wonderful beauty. Mistaken romance can easily occur in these instances. Look deeply into the mirror, "adorn yourself with beautiful robes and flowers" (*Early Docs.*, 48), and enter into your own loving gaze.

Perhaps we can learn from the medieval poet quoted at the beginning of this chapter as he writes that he can see both himself and his loved one. Not one or the other, but both. His gaze is complete as he witnesses both the truth and the radiance. May we learn to gaze with this same fullness.

Companion Meditation:
Drawing into the depth of your being, hold the mirror of conscious love before you. Let your gaze linger and take you where it will. See both the truth and the radiance that you are. Claim it all. Now turn your mirror to your companion. What do you see? Allow the truth of reflection to come back to you. See the eternal love, living both within yourself and in your companion.

Community Meditation:
Gathering together breathe into the very nature of truthfulness in your being. Do you live in truth? Does your community live in truth? Let the Spirit show you ways you may be covering this truth within. Open yourself to the radiance that is there and wants to be lived. Acknowledge it and claim it. Let it become part of your truth-living in the community. Let the community acknowledge its source of radiance and allow it be lived here and now on earth.

5

Love Gazing

Happy, indeed, is she ...
Whose contemplation refreshes.

—*The Lady,* 54–55

Contemplation was the great jewel for Clare. It allowed her gaze and soul to rest upon and within the infinite spheres of love. Here, her whole being was immersed and brought ever closer to a reality of existence that remains at a distance for most of us. The sisters who lived with her said that, when she returned from her time of prayer and contemplation, her face appeared clear and more beautiful and her words were filled with sweetness (*The Lady,* 163). She brought back gifts for all from the eternal place she had been taken to.

But what exactly is this contemplation that refreshed Clare, and how do we in our busy, noisy lives access its depths? Thomas of Celano, a follower and brother of St. Francis, gives us entry into the contemplative experience of Clare and her sisters. He wrote in 1228, "They have so merited the height of contemplation that they learn in it everything they should do or avoid, and they know with joy how to leave the mind for God" (*Early Docs.,* 257). Their experience, then, was one of both instruction and entrance into the Great Mystery and Silence. The former can bring peace of mind as to how to handle certain practical situations, but the latter is where real spiritual refreshment occurs.

Isaiah 18:4, tells us of the starting point, "I will take my rest and I will look on from my dwelling place." In the process of instruction, both the soul and the mind enter into an active listening and can bring back information and guidance. The next step is when we leave the mind for God—what joy! No wonder Clare relished her contemplative time. Giving her mind over to the Spirit, she was able to go beyond the small silence that we encounter in our meditations and enter into the Great Silence. This was where she moved beyond instruction into the depth of contemplation of the eternal.

Clare was diligent in her contemplative practice, and so must we be if we want to enter into the glories that not only wait for us but also call us. Can we even hear the call? Nehemiah 8:11 tells us, "Be still, for the day is holy." Every day is holy, every day we are called. Can we answer and gaze lovingly in silence? Can we leave the mind for God, even after all our years of meditating? If you cannot, do not become dismayed but simply bring yourself into the presence of Christ and offer your mind. Continue your daily practice, and let the Spirit bring you joy in its own way and time.

Clare and Francis spent more time gazing at God than they did gazing at each other. This is an important fact to remember as we struggle to free ourselves from romantic addictions. Contemplating one another in excess can only lead to illusion about love and unhealthy enmeshment. True contemplation of soul companions lies not with placing attention on each individual but rather with contemplating the Great Mystery that unites them. May we become like Clare and Francis, and dare to enter the infinity of such a loving gaze!

Companion Meditation:
Come into your place of quiet and bless your soul and bless your mind. Bless your companion and offer all to the Spirit of Christ. Let yourself joyfully descend into the depths of your being, and let love contemplate you. And now, contemplate love. Feel a joining with Christ in this love and with yourself. Feel a joining with your companion in this same love. Bless and love all.

Community Meditation:
Join as brothers and sisters in the breath of love, breathing as one body, one soul. Let the prayer of contemplation immerse you in this love. Open yourselves to any instructions that the Spirit wants to reveal to you. Open yourselves even more deeply to be immersed in the Great Silence. Let this be the very core of your community, from where all your actions, love, and living emerge.

6

Evoking Beauty

> *… that she might cling with her whole heart to*
> *Him Whose beauty all the blessed hosts of heaven*
> *unceasingly admire.*

—*The Lady*, 54

Our world is mesmerized by beauty, and it always has been. The reason for this is best articulated by Sister Frances Teresa, in *The Living Mirror*, "Beauty is our surest image of the loveliness of God, it is the only truly irresistible attraction. It is beauty which draws us, beauty which is the major current in our deepest ocean" (61). Beauty is, essentially, the deepest core of who we are. No wonder we are endlessly attracted to beauty—we are acknowledging the very source of the divine beauty within us all.

Clare was known to be particularly physically beautiful. And her beauty was seen as a great asset, which would make many noble lords (and there were many), willing to marry her. Clare, however, was not concerned with utilizing her "asset" for material comfort or gain. She reached beyond her vanity and pride, and even let Francis cut her long blond hair (a woman's most treasured possession). We usually consider vanity and pride to be intrinsic parts of our human nature, yet Clare has a different understanding; she writes, "the pride that destroys human nature, and the vanity that infatuates human hearts" (*The Lady*, 50). She is making a distinction here between our humanity and these "subtle enemies," which can only be overcome through the gift of wisdom coming from the "mouth of God" (Ibid.)

By clinging with our whole heart to this wisdom, that is, our inner Christ essence, we, like Clare, can enter into our humanness in its purest form and not be caught by those human enemies, pride and vanity. We can become like that man called Jesus, who knew he was the blessed and beautiful son of God and who lived his life from this knowledge. The lover writes in the Song of Songs 4:7 (NJ), "You are wholly beautiful, my love, and without a blemish." Those entering into the maturity of their soul are not led by mere physical attraction; they know beauty is revealed through both the inner and outer being. Those who are still bound to the outer vision of physicality, are still struggling with their immature selves, and are still seeking their own beauty through another.

Unfortunately, beauty has assumed a profoundly polluted role in our world. It has become a false idol based on imagery and form, and has been restricted to a superficial perception of the eye alone. It is the shadow, or shallow side of love, creating numerous anxieties and many disappointments in the realm of love. An Old Testament prophet's words are still applicable to us today: he claims, "You were the seal of perfection, full of wisdom and perfect in beauty" (Ezek. 28:12). He describes at length how this wisdom and perfection have been abused and how we have desecrated this great God-given gift: "At the entry of every valley you made yourself a high place, defiling your beauty" (Ezek. 16:25). Clare writes that believing in surface realities only causes our downfall from our original place of beauty. Our souls no longer shine with the beauty of our inner sun and moon, because all attention is placed upon the outer appearance.

To be in balance, however, attending to both our inner and our outer beings, is a responsibility we all have. Our health and bodies demand and deserve this balance, and it is no crime to wish to look one's best. The new lover pays attention to all aspects of his or her being—it is only with familiarity that we get a little sloppy and lazy. We enjoy the beauty around us in the natural world. Are we not also a part of that world? We can contribute to the enhancement of beauty, but deeper understanding is necessary for our beauty to bring real pleasure to another. That is, the attraction will be not a momentary, lustful arousal but recognition of the aliveness of the Spirit. We can all become, once more, true images of the loveliness of God, and we can all become witnesses of this as She walks by.

Companion Meditation:
Come into your breath and let yourself gently see your own divine beauty. Breathe deeply into this beauty. See what shallow notions of beauty may live within you—are they concerned with vanity or surface images? If so, hand them over to the truth of beauty and let them be blessed. How do you see your companion's beauty? Allow it to evolve into the purest form of vision.

Community Meditation:
How important is beauty to your community? Gathering in silence, let each breathe into the spirit of beauty. See how you may express this spirit within your community, whether through the visual arts, music, or through any other form. Bless your beauty and the beauty within all your community members, and let all contribute to a more mature and beautiful world.

7

Fidelity of the Gaze

Whose appearance is more beautiful,
... and has surrounded you with sparkling
gems as though blossoms of springtime

—***Early Docs.***, 35

One of the most common problems we encounter in our intimate relationships is the attention of our lover being diverted to another. It is as if an invisible net has been thrown over our lover's body and is drawing him or her towards the object of admiration. This awkward situation needs to be handled with great awareness by all persons involved. There is in this calling or drawing of attention, something to be revealed, and the mature person can follow this calling to find the truth that lies beneath.

Francis, once he devoted his life to God, was known for his restricted relations with women. Clare was his principal companion, and he had another woman friend, Jacopa, whom he claimed was his "brother." He constantly reminded the brothers when visiting and working with the sisters to take care not to let their gaze wander. He used this parable to explain his attitude: "There was a king who sent two messengers to his promised bride. The first returned and only told of his mission; the second expatiated at length on the beauty of the queen. The king called back the first messenger and asked, 'What of the queen? You have told me nothing about her.' 'Sire, she listened

to me in silence and with great attention.' 'But what of her beauty?'
'Sire, that is for you to judge; my task was to deliver your message.'"(De Robeck, 44)

And so Francis reminded his brothers that they were called to work
and offer assistance at the monastery, not to become enthralled by the
sisters' beauty. But what do we do when we feel that initial drawing of
attention? It is often experienced as an involuntary tug upon the gaze,
and there is a sense of lack of control in being drawn in such a way.
Here is where our discipline must rise to our aid, taking us into our
internal place of love, where we can ask, "What is this attraction?" If
we are still prone to the attractions of our lower nature, we could simply be at the mercy of our idea of physical beauty in its basest form
and our desire to possess, sexually or otherwise. Alternatively, the person to whom we are attracted could remind us of an unhealed love
wound that needs to be attended to. Or there may be something that
this soul is meant to reveal to our soul in order to bring us closer to
God, and a simple conversation could bear a great blessing. Only our
desire for truth will open the door to the greater reality at work.

Clare definitely desired truth and coming closer to God through
her relationships. Her views on the commingling of the brothers and
sisters were much more lenient than those of Francis. Perhaps the dis-
parity in their prior lives has something to do with this difference.
Francis, as we know, had been a reveler and no stranger to women.
Clare, by contrast, had no desire for anyone other than Francis, and
this desire was very different from his previous liaisons. Francis clearly
was taking no chances in preventing the brothers' thoughts from
becoming inflamed by the wrong sort of passion. Clare simply continued to live from the passion of her spirit.

Many may believe this is an impossible place to live from. And
perhaps one of the hardest sayings in the New Testament is Matthew
5:28: "But I say to you that whoever looks at a woman to lust for her
has already committed adultery with her in his heart." We are being
asked to raise the level of our consciousness so we that we may no

longer be imprisoned by our ingrained patterns of behavior. We are being asked to give birth to a greater harmony of loving.

Companion Meditation:
Come into the quietness of being and feel yourself flowing into the breath of love. Let it carry you. Then allow any experience of attraction to another to come into your awareness. See how you responded at the time. Then let the truth of that attraction speak to you. Bless the person involved, and let him or her go. Commit yourself to the truth of your being and to your companion.

Community Meditation:
Is your community faithful to its vision? Blessing your vision and all your members, come into the breath of love. Let the Spirit guide you in revealing the truth about your community vision. Are there areas that need to be lived more fully? Are there places where the Spirit is absent? Let the blessing of faithfulness rest upon you and all the community, and breathe deeply into this blessing. Let this faithfulness live within you.

Hearing: Love Songs

The time of singing has come,
And the voice of the turtledove
Is heard in our land.

—Song of Songs 2:12

Our voices carry the vibrations of our souls to our selves and to others. It is time for them to carry the tender vibration of love. It is the time of the turtledove. In this sense we are challenged to be truly present to ourselves, to look honestly at what we are carrying within and what we are placing into the world through our words.

Are we gentle with ourselves? Are we gentle with others? Where does our nourishment lie? True gentleness of soul can be birthed only through gentleness towards our own humanity. True nourishment lies in knowing what our soul most needs. Nourishment of our own self is usually the last need to which we attend, but our intimate lives demand it, our souls long for it, and our compassion for others can arise only when are grounded in the nourishment of compassion for ourselves. The invitation here is to love ourselves and others.

8

A New Love

To her who is half of her soul and the special
shrine of her heart's deepest love ... may she sing
the new song ... before the throne of God.

—***The Lady***, 54

We are being called to put aside our old beliefs, whether they come from personal experience or generational inheritance, about the way we love and the way we relate to love. It is time to sing our way into a new existence where the mystery of love becomes a reality in our everyday living. We can do this by celebrating love's mysterious beauty every morning, and by not falling into a repetitive, lifeless motion in which we think we already know what is the outcome. Too often this foreseen outcome is nothing more than a projection of past painful experiences onto a fearful future. The way to a new love, being lived in and through the presence of God and self, is now openly inviting us. To be in this presence is to be in the fullness of intimacy, a blessed pathway to walk.

In the quotation that opens this chapter, Clare is alluding to The Book of Revelation to John (14:3-4), in which a vision for a new life is given, with harpists playing and a new song being sung in honor of God. When she writes, "to her who is half of her soul," she is referring to our humanity, that is, saying our human soul is only half of our fullness. She then joins these words with "the special shrine of her heart's deepest love," which is the holy seat of our divinity. Clare was a great lover of both the human and the divine Jesus. This union made sense to her, both mystically and rationally, and allowed for her own humanity and divinity to come into their fullness. In this unity, God composed the new love song, the new vision of love, within and through her. And it kept growing within her every day. She asks us to open to this same possibility.

In what ways do we deny the new love song being sung through us? Do we even think that a new way of loving is possible, or are we still carrying shards of pain within our hearts? It is vital that we see what old beliefs we are still clinging to in the depths of our being. They need the light of the Spirit to show whether they are truly viable—and we need only ask the Spirit for that insight. The real question is, Do we want to know those beliefs for what they are, or do we want to keep singing the old tune of a forsaken love? Sometimes holding onto our old perceptions is easier than being completely open and vulnerable to our hearts.

Clare removed all traces of her old life when she joined Francis. No doubt she grieved deeply as she left the only home she'd ever known, the love of her family and those in her intimate community. She could not have contained this grief and moved forward into a new life at the same time. Her pain must have been sung in those initial dark nights of not knowing where she was to go. And she must have felt great confusion and even more pain at Francis moving her from place to place and leaving her alone in this transitional time. Perhaps that was the purpose of this difficult time—to empty herself before the shrine of God, so that she could be filled with the presence of the greater love.

To fully come into our presence, we must be entirely honest with all that we feel. We are not to indulge in the feelings, but neither are we to deny them. They must be expressed in the dark of the night in order for the sun of love to rise. We must let go of the harsh memories we treasure and guard with our lives (literally), and make way for the real pearls of love to fall into our hearts. In this way, the new mystical song of love can make its home in our inner sanctuary.

May we, like Clare, learn to empty ourselves and come into the utterly unknowable place of love. May we reach into our human and divine fullness and allow the new mysterious love song to touch us deeply and pour forth from our hearts to all those around us.

Companion Meditation:
Come into the quiet of your being and allow yourself to drop deeply into your inner sanctuary. Allow any old grief to arise, whether it concerns your family, companion, or a past love. Ask for the light of love to shine on this grief and allow it to pour forth from your being, whether silently or in the form of sound, song, or even dance. Let yourself be emptied by the spirit of love, and sit in that emptiness. Bless all involved. When it is time, you will be filled with a new song of life and love.

Community Meditation:
Is your community singing a new song of love for the world to hear? Coming together into the utterly unknowable love, place your community in its loving arms. Listen to the song of your community as it is now. Listen even more deeply to the new song waiting to be sung, which the world wants to hear. How can you all join together in this new love song?

9

Jewels of the Soul

*In your love may the tongue of the flesh
be silent; may the tongue of the Spirit
speak.*

—***The Lady,*** *57*

In our contemporary Western society, words and language have been relegated to a purely perfunctory role. Except in the realm of poets, the sacred poetic nature of our speech and its ability to reveal the truth of our souls has been forsaken. Other cultures—African, Middle Eastern, and Celtic, to name a few—still bring forward their inner soul nature through poetic language in everyday conversation. They know the word is alive with sacredness and truth.

In Europe during the Middle Ages, troubadours provided an ethos of musicality and poetic songs. The air was filled with love ballads guaranteed to stir the heart and soul, and these were, no doubt, a great influence on Francis and his spontaneous love songs for God. Clare's poetic nature is clearly present in her writings, in particular her letters. In these works she reveals her soul without hesitation as she weaves her relationship with God and Francis into what we might call a love treatise. She also frequently refers to the Psalms, ancient expressions of the soul, which on numerous occasions were sung and accompanied with musical instruments. The physical ear became the conduit to arouse the heart of the listener, and the soul was the author of the account of the love journey to be heard.

How often do we truly reveal the nature of our souls? Our days are filled with superficial greetings and meetings, where the soul has no business, or so we think. Revealing our feelings has been quite a popular fad; however, we have discovered that these feelings can change as the wind changes. When people believe they need to encounter and discuss every feeling that arises, their relationships quickly become tedious and tiring. This is especially so in a whole community! A feeling can persuade us that it is a definitive truth, but we have also seen the folly in this delusion, as we have witnessed a feeling dissolve in a moment of alternative explanation. Feelings can damage relationships or at least cause confusion when "the tongue of the flesh" expresses their perceived belief. Let the tongue of the flesh be silent, Clare writes, and let the spirit speak.

In order for the spirit to speak, we must reach back into the sacredness of the word, the Eternal Word and Breath, as spirit and truth, and become conduits for their manifestation on earth. It is no use entering into this spirit alone and hiding it from others. We must come forward, just as Clare and Francis came forward, just as Jesus walked the length of Palestine bringing that Eternal Word and Breath into life. Jesus had his way of conveying this Word, and Clare had hers. We too are called to let our language become an infectious expression of who we are in the deepest place of our souls, that place that only God sees. Now is the time for our words to become the jewels of our souls, and to allow their glory to be uncovered for all to see.

Companion Meditation:
Breathing into your place of stillness, let all words and thoughts come to rest. Witness how you use language in your daily life—does it express your deepest self? Do your words express the depth and breadth of your love for your companion? Ask the Spirit to show you the Eternal Word and Breath within, and breathe from here. Continue breathing in and from this place. Gradually let your words emerge from here, in truth and spirit.

Community Meditation:
Does your community speak in spirit and truth? Let all gather with the intent to deepen the communication of the soul. Let yourselves breathe into the Eternal Word, coming into the depths of your spirit. Let breath and words of the spirit mingle until there is no separation. Let only these words pass your lips as you end the meditation.

10

Tender Words

I beg you to receive my words
with kindness and devotion.

—*The Lady*, 57

The harshness of our world can easily creep into our communication.
Our innate tenderness is placed aside as we struggle for soul survival
in a seemingly soulless world. Our strength appears to lie in the development of an impenetrable defense, but this appearance is an illusion.
It is time to return to our tenderness, to a softness of heart and
response, with the blessing of an underlying firmness of love. This was
the way of Clare. This was Clare.

She was adamant with her sisters about the nature of speech; it was
to be entered into with the utmost awareness. Clare wrote that "care-
less speech always weakens our love" (De Robeck, 88–89) and that
any unrestrained talk causes the mind to dart here and there, quickly
falling into frivolous and sometimes harmful conversation. She found
gossip or the speaking of others in their absence especially destructive.
Such talk affects both the speaker and the listener, tainting their souls
with a superior malice, and also draws both parties into a false sense of
companionship. And the one being spoken of is alienated from the
others involved.

Such speaking of another and her or his annoying or quirky ways
seems to relieve a pressure that can otherwise build to a nasty out-

pouring of words. But this pressure comes from nothing more than believing the judgments of our minds. Allowing another simply to be is a great gift. And if something needs to be communicated, let us follow Clare in conveying our words carefully, with tenderness and love. If words are sent with angry barbs, then our old armor can reemerge. If the arrow of love is aimed towards us, we are given the opportunity to open our heart and melt into the truth of what is being said. Real communication is always entered into and received with love.

What if you find yourself shooting out those barbs even when you do not want to? Then it is time for some soulful investigation. As a rendition of NJ Luke 6:45 may say, "For a woman's words flow out of what fills her heart." What is the real source of this type of communication? Was it your family's way of speaking? Are you afraid to let go of your own armor for fear that real loving communication may touch your heart? Is a past wound being touched? Only you and the Spirit know, and only you and the Spirit together can bring you back into the original tender words of your love.

Similarly, we must be conscious of how we are receiving the words of others. The quotation of Clare that opens this chapter begins with "I beg you": "I beg you to receive my words with kindness and devotion." Clare understood the importance of how we hear others, and how we receive their words. A misunderstanding of intent or a misheard arrow of truth can very easily turn our hearts away from the one delivering a message of love. And this turning away can evolve into a hardening of the heart and a distance that causes pain to all. Until we turn back in love, the distance will continue to grow; we are always either moving towards or moving away from love.

If we do receive the arrow of truth in love, we may not like what we hear, but we recognize it as a gift. It is love calling us closer to itself. If another's words are filled with a nasty sting but we do not respond with defensive remarks or hide behind our armor, then love is standing firmly within us. Our tender words of love can then speak.

May we all strive for this tenderness of speech and loving communication. Our world needs gentle words and ways. As Jesus said in the

Beatitudes, "Blessed are the gentle, they shall have the earth for their heritage" (NJ Matt. 5:4). May we leave a gentle world as our children's and grandchildren's inheritance.

Companion Meditation:
Coming into your inner place of love, let yourself rest, away from all the harshness of the world. See how your soul may be tainted by this harshness. See how your speech to your companion and others may also be colored. How do you receive their words? Let your soul be cleansed, and let your words be filled with a tender love.

Community Meditation:
How do you speak to one another as a community? Are your words filled with a loving gentleness, or is another mode at work? Let all come into the gentleness of being and breathe into its presence. Let it soak into your soul. May there be awareness in your speech as you honor each person, by speaking and listening with tenderness, and allow yourself and all persons to gently be who they are.

11

Silent Times

*Do not wonder at all or think that the fire
of love for you glows with less delight ... No,
this is the difficulty: the lack of messengers
and the obvious dangers of the road.*

—*The Lady*, 54

"Speech is of time; silence is of eternity." These are the words of an anonymous contemporary Poor Clare sister. She also writes, "Silence is the ever-available but seldom-possessed treasure of those who are wise enough and humble enough to receive it" (Interior Prayer, Archival Material, Little Portion Friary, Long Island, NY). Through this wisdom and humility, we are taken into the eternal silence, into the infinite spaciousness, where no form or image exists. This is the place of deep rest. Only as we return to time and place, must shapes and colors and words appear, to reflect, ever so dimly, our experience.

In the letter quoted at the opening of this chapter, Clare reassures Agnes that the infrequency of her correspondence does not indicate a lack of love. She points to the common hindrance in those times of unreliable modes of delivery. I, however, invite an internal, metaphorical reading of the second sentence of this passage: that is, we may be encountering an internal danger of wandering from the Spirit, and the soul may need to be taken into its core of self-knowledge and healing. Alternatively, we may be entering the eternal depths of space and silence. Both of these places are solitary. When the moment arises for us to step back into time, messengers become available, and we can give our experience form through words or other means of expression. It is important that both our companions and we ourselves honor these times of silence, so that the divine illumination may be given to our souls. Shattering the silence before God's work is done can leave us in a profound state of both internal and external agitation. Evelyn Underhill wrote, "Silence is my home." May we not stop others, or ourselves, as we make these journeys home, and may we not misinterpret the ensuing silence as lost love.

Clare had a profound respect for silence. She was known for her abstemious use of words, and the daily life that she created for the sisters honored this valuing of silence in its rhythm of prayer and work. She said, "silence keeps us close to God" (De Robeck, 88–89). Silence is also that delicate space between lovers. Rumi writes,

> *"No more words. In the name of this place we drink in*
> *with our breathing, stay quiet like a flower.*
> *So the nightbirds will start singing"* (32).

This is that infinite space where we meet God, where eternal songs are audible only to the soul. Let us drink in these songs of love and, like the saints, become intoxicated by the divine love illuminated through ourselves and our companions. The great beauty of this space is that it is open to us all, as friends, as lovers, as community. The nightbirds are always there, waiting to sing to whoever will breathe into the silence.

Companion Meditation:
Come into the stillness of your being, and let yourself be immersed in the silence. Let go, and merge with the Great Silence. You are infinitely loved here. Let yourself go even deeper. Enter the infinite spaciousness of this love. Meet yourself here. Meet your companion here. And love.

Community Meditation:
Does the spirit of silence live within the soul of your community?
Invite the spirit of the Great Silence to come and dwell within your souls.
Breathe into the love of this silence and sigh into yourselves. Hear the
nightbirds singing. Hear the nightbirds of your community singing. Bring
back those songs for all to hear, in whatever form they want to be
expressed.

12

Humble Discernment

*If anyone would tell you something else or suggest
something that would hinder your perfection or seem
contrary to your divine vocation, even though you
must respect him, do not follow his counsel.*

—***Early Docs.***, 41

On our spiritual journey we reach many crossroads with decisions
needing to be made, and consequently, the need for discernment
through prayer and the counsel of others. These times may arise in a
number of ways: with a crystal-like clarity; with a gentle leaning in a
particular direction; or with murkiness and confusion. A little doubt
is good for the soul, because it keeps us in a place of humility and
openness to the true nature of the divine will. Too much doubt is dis-
orienting; too much certainty is spiritual arrogance; and confusion is
the voice of the ego doing battle with God. Sometimes we need help
in discerning what we are experiencing.

The one fear Francis had was of his own will. He was particularly
drawn to "the life of the angels," or the life of prayer and contemplation, and was considering becoming a hermit. He was also, however,
leaning towards a life of preaching. He took this divine riddle to the
one person he trusted implicitly—Clare. She then took it to the One
she trusted without question. Her prayer revealed that Francis was to
preach, and he, without hesitation, strode into the world (De Robeck,

47). This is just one of many instances when Francis visited Clare for spiritual solace and counsel.

How easy it would have been for Clare to let her own desires influence her advice. By conveying to Francis that he was to preach, she was effectively sending him away. As a hermit he would have been close by and would have ministered to the sisters as teacher and spiritual adviser. But Clare, by living in the truth of her spirit, was able to communicate the truth for Francis. When our companions ask for counsel, can we exercise such personal abandon? In order to hear the truth, we must be sitting in openness, without our own ideas or desires interfering.

On one occasion, Francis sent four women to Clare, asking her to accept them as members of her community. Clare, after speaking with the women agreed to accept three of them but felt the fourth was not suited to the community life. Francis disagreed and virtually insisted that Clare accept her. Clare acquiesced. After six troublesome months, that woman left the community.

In this instance, Francis thought he was seeing with greater clarity than Clare. Perhaps she knew the outcome all along? Perhaps she bowed down to Francis knowing the truth would come eventually to light, or perhaps she entered into self-doubt? We do not know which. But as it is said in Matthew 8:16, "You will know them by their fruits."

In coming into a sacred trust with our companions, we must also remember that the ultimate discernment resides with ourselves, no matter how advanced the other is. After all, we all have our blind spots. This is the test of true companionship. Are we able to open ourselves to the counsel of another without being swayed from our own inner guidance? Can we discern when to listen to another and when to listen to ourselves? And in giving counsel, are we able to bow down when the other decides differently from what we have suggested? Humility is key in the discerning process.

May we all pray that the strength of our inner love and discernment will grow with each moment and with every prayer, producing fruits for the good of all.

Companion Meditation:
Flowing into the breath of the Spirit let yourself be taken beyond your own will. Allow yourself to come into the tender divine will. See yourself and your life from this place. Let all discernment come from here. Breathe into the companionship you have with God, and let that be the foundation for the love between you and your companion.

Community Meditation:
How does your community discern its decisions? Come together and let each one breathe deeply within. Let go of personal views and opinions. Move beyond to the greater Spirit of knowing. Let the heat of the Spirit move through you and bring forward the silence, or words, as given. Designate a time of sharing if desired.

13

Lullabies of Love

[we] want and [have] absolute need of
heavenly nourishment

—*Early Docs.,* 36

The love and nourishment that we need is often found in the most simple of gestures—an encouraging word, a gentle love song, a physical embrace. We are, through these gestures, held in tenderness and experience a reassurance that we are loved. These are beautiful moments that we all cherish. Unfortunately, in our busy and self-reliant world, we seek out such comfort only when in dire need. We must come to realize that an inherent part of our nature needs to be nourished regularly, not just in soul emergencies.

Clare's letters were certainly "heavenly nourishment" for Agnes as she contended with the initiation of a new community. Though Agnes's letters did not survive, it is obvious that Clare was responding to concerns Agnes was facing. No doubt Clare's words soothed Agnes back into the heart of love and provided much-needed encouragement to continue her chosen life. Clare also gave generously to her sisters, spiritually, emotionally, and physically. In *The Testament* we read how she would tend to the ill sisters, bathing their wounds and bodies, and washing the feet of those who returned tired and dusty from their travels. She reprimanded, when necessary, with gentle words and always made herself available to any who wished for her counsel. She was as a mother with her children, caring for them within the divine womb, and cradling them in love.

Clare herself also received support and nourishment from her sisters. She writes of the joy she feels through having her mother, sister, and other family and friends with her at San Damiano (they all eventually joined her community). But of course, it was Francis who, above all other living beings on earth, provided her spiritual nourishment. Their understanding of each other's spiritual lives brought Clare deep soul contentment, as did their brief physical meetings. Francis's absence was not so easy for her to contend with. Sometimes he would send the brothers to her, and they would sing songs that Francis had composed. It must have been a sweet pain to hear his soulful compositions yet simultaneously be aware of his physical absence.

I wonder what songs Clare and Francis sung in their precious moments of togetherness? What great lullabies of love did they enter to join their souls with God, to reassure each other with holy calm?

We would do well to find our own lullaby and then offer it to our companions and community and any others we meet along the way. Every day the divine calm calls for us to sing its song. We may think we are too busy or too tired, yet this is our real sustenance and nourishment. The bride and bridegroom in the Song of Songs knew this secret: "I hear my love ... [He] lifts up his voice, he says to me, 'Come then, my beloved, my lovely one, come ... let me hear your voice; for your voice is sweet ...'" (NJ 2:8, 10, 14). The voice of another becomes the voice of God when it is infused with such love. May we be that for one another in this world and the world to come. May we learn both to sing and be sung to.

Companion Meditation:
With your companion, come into your breath of love, let yourself reach down to feel the wonderful and tender love you have for your companion. Let it flow through the whole of your being. Let it overflow into a gentle song, words of love, or into a deep embrace. Hold your companion in and

through this love, nourishing her being, nourishing your love for him. (If alone, do this meditation for yourself.)

Community Meditation:
How does your community nourish itself? Joining together, come into the depths of love. Let yourselves be taken into the tender nourishment of God as Mother. Fold into her gentle and loving arms and be cradled and divinely sung to. Ask yourself how the members of your community may do this for yourselves and for one another?

14

One Song

*Let us respond
with one voice,
with one spirit*

—***Early Docs.***, 49

Our world has been split into many factions: political, religious, economic, and racial. Our inner world is also experienced as separate parts of being: logic, intuition, feeling, ego, and our inner God. Maturity brings our internal being into a blessed state of equanimity and unity with the whole of our self. When this occurs, our external world has a chance of experiencing unity also.

Every day we are given the opportunity to develop into mature beings. We are given various situations, at work or at home, in which beliefs and prejudices beg to be looked at compassionately. Often we do not even know we are carrying attitudes that can cause judgment and, ultimately, deep discontentment. They separate us from life and distance us from our community, our companions, our own inner love. We become icons of isolation. Many today feel desolate, even in the midst of their families and friends. Suicide rates, addictions, violence, and pervasive loneliness are all shouting this separation to us.

Clare and Francis knew well the discontent of a world living in separation. In their lifetime it was the wide gap between the rich and the poor. They knew that this division did not need to exist, and that wealth does not bring inner happiness. Only in drawing all together in love could any sense of harmony and happiness be lived. Clare and Francis knew that God is everywhere upon this earth, not just in the church (as many of that time believed) but also in the poor woman weaving, in the birds flying in the air and the flowers that spread across the hills. All were part of the one song of love.

Francis, towards the end of his life, made his way to Clare. She had a special hut built in the garden at San Damiano and took care of him. He was experiencing excruciating bodily and soul pain, and she soothed them both. From this darkness came the Canticle of Brother Sun, the celebrated song in which Francis acknowledges the earth and all the elements as mother, sister, and brother. He sings praises to the Creator for all that is given and reminds us that the one who lives in peace, forgiveness, and humility can know and embody the divine will. In this way, life will be lived in harmony and Sister Death will be welcomed. Did Clare and Francis sing this canticle together as Sister Moon made her night journey, or as Brother Sun shone on the morning dew? Those were precious and secret days and nights together, I am sure.

Rainer Maria Rilke in his "Sonnets to Orpheus," captures, I think, what Clare and Francis were giving birth to:

> *"For song, as taught by you, is not desire,*
> *not wooing of something finally attained;*
> *song is existence …*
> *… It's more than being in love …*
> *… learn to forget those fleeting ecstasies.*
> *Far other is the breath of real singing. An aimless breath. A stirring in the*
> *god"* (131).

There is a forgetting of the self when one enters into the grander self of love and existence—here is where unity is known and separation and isolation cease to exist.

May we learn to expand in such a way, moving from the greed and domination of an "I" and "me" culture to encompass the reality of our unity. Until we are all included, we will be separate. Until we learn to love and sing the one song, we will be lonely.

Companion Meditation:
Joining with your companion, find a holy song of love, a chant, or a blessing that speaks of unity and companionship. Bring yourselves into a deep space of love and simple being through your breath. Letting the Spirit inspire, one may begin the chosen song, the other may join whenever ready. Sing or chant for a good period of time, allowing your voices to be filled with the Spirit, coming together in unity and love.
(If alone, do this meditation by coming into unity with self and God).

Community Meditation:
Does your community have a song or chant symbolizing unity? If so, is it still meaningful? If not, choose a song that is appropriate to your community's vision. Bring yourselves together in love and spend time breathing into this love. Then let the Spirit sing through you, renewing your voice and commitment to your community and a unified world in love. Let your song be heard by all.

Smell: God's Perfume

Spiritual life is the bouquet, the perfume,
the flowering and fulfillment of a human
life.

—Joseph Campbell

Our sense of smell can be a powerful stimulant. It can also be very soothing, and can assist in gently opening the heart to other dimensions of loving. Our world is in dire need of returning to its sensual nature, and of allowing the body to be a conduit for spiritual expansion and evolution. This sense invites us to enter into this holy place of love and ritual. We are also asked to look deeply within, to those places where we refuse to embody the great love that we are offered and choose instead the limiting patterns of our past.

Let every meditation for this sense be prepared in a special way, with incense or the burning of essential oils. Allow yourself to open through the body and to receive the wisdom you innately carry.

15

Frankincense and Myrrh

*Happy, indeed, is she to whom it is given
to drink at this sacred banquet.*

—The Lady, 54

Rituals abound in our everyday lives, with or without our being conscious of their existence. When we enter into a ritual unconsciously, it loses its sacredness and power and becomes a routine obligation. The life force of that action is no longer stimulated, and a deadening of the soul ensues. We then can either act with rote soulless behavior or drop the ritual altogether. This loss of vital connection with ritual is very common today as the sacredness of everyday living is forgotten and the birthing of love reduced to a few special moments. It is time to remember that love is special in every moment; it is an ever-growing blessing that wants to be continuously born. Entering consciously into a ritual of love allows this birth to take place and to be honored and received.

When Jesus was born, his human and divine sacredness of being was acknowledged by the tenderness of his parents' love and the gifts of gold, frankincense, and myrrh. Mary and Joseph were conscious of who they were birthing into the world. Gabriel had delivered the incarnation message, and Elizabeth (Mary's relative and the expectant mother of John the Baptist) further confirmed this proclamation as the Holy Spirit opened her mind and John leapt with joy in her womb (Luke 1:41–45). Gestation time can be a period of deep awareness and connection. We can only open our imaginations to the communication that occurred between Mary, Joseph, and the spirit of Jesus waiting to be born.

The wise men bringing their ritualistic gifts of gold, frankincense, and myrrh were deemed wise because they were conscious of their actions. They were not simply wandering in the desert laden with gold artifacts and precious powders. They understood the impact of Jesus' birth; they were ritualistically honoring his divine wisdom and how it was to be awoken in others.

The birth of Jesus was the most celebrated occasion in the community of Clare and Francis. They, like the wise men, knew the grand implications of such an offering. They also knew that it was not a once-a-year blessing, to be cherished and then forgotten. This birthing of love is eternal. And one must come to this birthing consciously. It is not a place to come to with expectation of gaining treasures and then departing. No, this is a sacred place where one is given the invitation to open with awareness, and to drink with gratitude. In this way the soul is filled with divine grace and remembers its natural state of being. This is the ritual of love.

This love ritual can take many forms. We can become more aware of our actions, even within everyday activities. Rather than go on "automatic," we can bring an enlivened presence to what we do, noticing and appreciating the small details that help make up our existence. We can become mindful of our thoughts and words. We can watch and listen to see if they are filled with love for both ourselves and others. We can become conscious of our relating with companions and friends.

Is love being born by your being with another? Does your heart open to an even greater expansiveness through your interaction? Is the divine wisdom growing in you and in those you are in relationship with? If not, it is time to enter into a conscious love ritual, through intent, communication, breath, and prayer. In this way you will find the ritual that is suitable for you. And let the ritual change as you change. Do not seek a permanent method or rule. Love has no formula. Let its fluidity flow from one moment to the next.

Companion Meditation:
Coming into your breath, let yourself sink deeply into your own birthing place of love. Do you know this place? Keep letting yourself sink deeper. Ask that you may come to know what it is to give birth to love. Ask the Spirit to show you the way, and let your soul follow. Be open to discovering a special ritual of love with yourself and with your companion. Light the frankincense and myrrh, and above all, love!

Community Meditation:
How important is ritual to your community? Are your rituals alive and filled with divine grace? Coming into the community breath, let each person enter into his or her own ritualized body and spirit. Do you bring an enlivened presence to your worship, to your work in the community, to your communication? Let the Spirit take you to the sacred birthing place and show you the rituals of love. Learn to open to grace and receive with gratitude.

16

Sense Resurrection

Happy, indeed, is she ...
... Whose fragrance brings the dead to
life again.

—**The Lady**, 55

Our society has lost touch with the sensual nature of our beings. Busy schedules, extended work hours, and a multiplicity of errands have come to dominate our time. Our bodies and wholeness of being suffer as a result. By nature we are sensual creatures, and we need to tend and feed this part of ourselves just as frequently as we do our bellies. It is time to bring our senses back into life. In order to do this, we need to give dedicated time to this resurrection, reclaim the lost art of pleasure, and open ourselves to a renewed understanding of sensual eroticism.

Clare, in her writings, liberally uses all the senses to describe her relationship with God; she also uses the senses to teach others how to come into divine intimacy. She does not shy away from the fullness of her self in relating to her divine lover: she longingly looks upon her God, and his gaze meets hers; she listens and hears the Beloved's voice, and he does what she wishes when she calls; she delights in the divine fragrance that brings her soul to life, and this same fragrance, making its home in her, brings other souls to life; she tastes the divine nectar, and God himself in the banquet of her spirit; she reaches out and touches his love, and is caressed and held in return. This is her God's greatest pleasure.

Many mystics who have chosen a life of celibacy develop very sensual and erotic relationships with their Creator. This type of relating, however, is by no means only for the celibate. In fact, the mystics are showing us a beautiful pathway to God, and a way we can love and enjoy another.

Sensuality and eroticism have been erroneously branded as opposed to, or distinct from, spiritual love or agape. This opposition, however, exists only when we separate these forms of love. That is, if we choose only the sensual or erotic, that is what we will be given. When all forms—the sensual, erotic, and spiritual—coexist and are honored and lived in the fullness of one another, then we can begin to see God in our partners through all these paths.

Clare, as far as we know, did not enter into the physicality of her spiritual eroticism, but I believe that she felt strongly the potential for a sensual partnership with Francis. No wonder he was afraid! A woman's ardor can be a very threatening thing when lived in the fullness of God. As Hafiz writes (Ladinsky, 89),

> *"Fire has a love for itself—*
> *It wants to keep burning.*
>
> *It is like a woman*
> *Who is at last making love*
> *To the person she most desires."*

Whether we are in partnership or not, we can develop our sensual and erotic nature. We can resurrect these natural attributes from the dead. When we do so, the fullness of life awaits us. Many of us, though, fear that this part of ourselves will lead us into trouble. And so it can if it is not aligned with our spirit. But in coming into the Spirit, and bringing the sensual and erotic alongside, we have nothing to fear, only perhaps a pleasure that we did not know possible in this human existence. May we all discover this pleasure. May we all discover what our souls and bodies truly love.

Companion Meditation:
Come to this meditation with the intent of connecting deeply with Spirit.
Breathe in and through your whole being, breathe out and through your
whole being. Connect with all that you are. Open yourself to feel the
promptings of your spirit and your body. What, in this moment, would
give you the greatest of pleasures? Do not shy away from anything. Let
come whatever comes. Allow yourself the freedom to explore with yourself
and your companion.

Community Meditation:
In what ways do your community worship and meetings feed your sensual
nature? Gathering together in the quiet, let there be openness to the new.
Let there be openness to the sensuality of the spirit. May all feel safe to
come into Spirit with every part of their being, and breathe deeply into
this place within. Keep breathing, and find the rhythm of your body and
breath. Let Spirit show each one how the sensuality of spirit may feed all.

17

Deep Longing

Draw me after you,
let us run in the fragrance
of your perfumes

—*The Lady*, 57

In this quotation, which alludes to the Song of Songs, Clare, like
many mystics, recognizes and celebrates this elaborate and erotic love
poem as it speaks of her experience of love. It conveys what it is like to
be drawn out of oneself, running away from one's reasonable senses as
love lures one closer to union with the Beloved. And yet, there is also
the *desire* to be drawn, to run free, and to take delight in the sweet fragrance of love. There is a willingness to be captured by the Beloved, to
know more of what this love really is.

There are many forms of love in this life, and if we are living with
open hearts, we can experience love in an infinite number of ways.
Clare's love for Francis opened into places that few people dare to go.
It was a love that called to her with a deep spiritual longing, drawing
her mind, body, and soul into a continual wave of spirit companionship. She experienced the yearning of her mind to speak with him; the
need of her body to be close to him; and the craving of her soul to
love him. These longings were all beautifully bound together and
came forth from the spiritual foundation of her love for God. Yes, she
wanted to run free in the fragrance of their love. Leaving her family

home, she was not afraid of what others would say, or of her reputation being tarnished. She ran in the middle of the night, following the perfume of love, not only daring to answer the call, but also courageously calling love to her. How many of us are so bold? How many of us run the other way?

When we experience such a strong attraction to another, we can fall into the need to be together with a kind of madness. The questions are, What exactly is being taken over? And who or what is now in charge? Reason is the first of our attributes to make an exit when love makes an entry. And reason is followed closely by rules, laws, and other people's judgments. Our restrictive thoughts and behaviors, based on 'cultural order,' bind us to a false safety and stop true love from prying open our hearts and pouring itself in. Very often it is the closed heart that this love takes over. But who is calling us beyond ourselves? What is this insanity that is stirring our former comfortable lives? "Who is this coming out of the wilderness/Like pillars of smoke?"(Song of Songs 3:6). We are so easily foiled by the little foxes that spoil the vineyards (Song of Songs 2:15), that is, all the thoughts in the mind, which can stop love developing and invite confusion in as we seek to discern the true nature of the love we are feeling.

A deep commitment to love the self is required to truly answer the questions in the preceding paragraph. In loving yourself, in seeking the best for your whole being, trust that the truth will emerge. When we fall in love, we need to pay attention to our human weaknesses: if you tend to become clouded by pure physical passion, then know this and be aware; if your soul is partial to seeking love through codependency, then pay close attention to this inclination; if you fall outrageously in love over and over again, then take care. We all have our weak spots that can be projected onto others, and this projection can create a false urgency.

But what of Clare's deep longing? Can we not also enter into such a genuine experience? Of course we can. As we commit ourselves to the fullness of our own beings, aligning mind, body, and soul in the foundation of spirit, we learn to open to the truth and maturity of love within our selves and with another. Then our longing for another is with our whole being, not just a part of who we are. Certainly needs and projections may also be present, but with real love, the greater commitment purifies these desires, renewing soul and spirit together. Through this renewal, the urgency to be with another transforms into a continual reawakening and is felt to the core of one's being, with the heart opening in profound ways.

May we follow Clare into the depth of longing, and may we come into the holy garden of real love: "How fragrant your perfumes, more fragrant than all other spices ... Breathe over my garden to spread its sweet smell around" (NJ Song of Songs 4:10, 16).

Companion Meditation:
Breathe into the very depths of your body. Breathe in and through your mind. Let your breath permeate every part of your soul. Align this breath, your body, mind, and soul, with your spirit, and the spirit of love. What is the most important thing for you right now? What do you need to do to commit to your being and love of self? Share this with your companion.

Community Meditation:
Is your heart being opened, and is your soul growing through your involvement with your community? Come together in love, and let your breath flow through your body, into your mind, and let it fill the whole of your soul. Allow the spirit of the great love to connect with your spirit and the spirit of your community. Be open to know if this is the right community for you at this time.

18

Love Disguised

*[I see, too] that by humility, the virtue of faith,
and ... poverty, you have taken hold of that
incomparable treasure hidden in the field of the
world and of the human heart.*

—Early Docs., 44

For Clare, humility, faith, and poverty were necessary attributes to live fully in love. Humility she understood as not placing oneself above another—any other, regardless of social or financial status, and irrespective of the state of the other's soul or consciousness. Faith for Clare was a complete trust in the divine love and tenderness, in the most painful moments and in the joyful revelations. Poverty was an acknowledgment that without God we are all poor.

Clare lived and breathed these virtues even before her meeting with Francis. She was known to seek out the lepers who were banished to the outer areas of Assisi, to feed and care for them. This was a task that few would undertake, but Clare, feeling compassion in her soul for those in greatest need, did not hesitate in loving them in the ways they most needed. First, she acknowledged and respected their soul beings, seeing the hidden beauty within their decimated bodies. Then she tended to those bodies with her own hands. She did not keep the divine tenderness only for those pleasing to her sight or smell but abandoned the delicacy of her upbringing to give the love that God had so lavishly given to her.

God does not differentiate between those who live on the edges and those who have been accepted by society, nor should we. Clare did not make this distinction either, and this is why the monastic order of the Poor Clares spread so rapidly through Europe even while she was alive. We are inherently compassionate, with a great deal of love for one another. We simply need to learn how to communicate this love with every being we meet, regardless of situation or soul difficulties. Love overrides all categories, all wealth, and all ill health.

What do we do when our partners or community members go to the outer edges of their being? That is, how do we respond when, straying from the centers of their souls, they enter into the less attractive parts of themselves? Do we reject them, ignore them, or try to change them? Or can we, like Clare, see that incomparable treasure hidden in the fields of their human hearts and hold them in the depth of love and compassion? If we are able to do the latter, without trying to do anything else, we will witness the return of our companions to their compassionate and loving selves. Like begets like. Love begets love. There is nothing more to be done, nothing to be fixed or changed. Love can take care of itself.

In the Gospel of Philip it is written, "Whoever is free of the world can no longer be made into a slave there. They have risen above attraction and repulsion. They are master of their nature" (91). Our world has miseducated us in many ways, very persuasively defining what is deemed attractive. To be free from this limiting definition is to be free from the slavery of what also repulses us. Francis, unlike Clare, was repulsed by the lepers, but he came to recognize that this place of repulsion was where he most needed to learn how to love. He therefore devoted his time to caring for the lepers, and eventually, without changing or curing them, he saw the Christ within each one. Through this new perception he knew he was given the gift of freedom and love.

May we learn to simply love one another, going beyond our superficial attractions and repulsions and desires for others to change, and come to see the treasure that is in every heart and in the entire world.

Companion Meditation:
Coming into your breath, let yourself fall deeply into the breath of love. Allow to arise any traits in your companion that you find difficult or want to change. Breathe the breath of love in and through these places and keep breathing. Hold the traits and your companion in the arms of total compassion and love. Let the Spirit dissolve any difficulties you may have in doing this, and let love beget love. (If you are alone, do this meditation for any self-difficulties you perceive, or for a friend.)

Community Meditation:
Do your community members come from varied social and financial backgrounds? Are there many pathways and traditions represented in your community? If yes, how can you come into a greater acceptance and love of one another? If not, how can you open your doors wider? Coming into the stillness together, let the Spirit move in and through the breath of your community and each individual soul, opening the heart of compassion and understanding. Allow the Spirit to show you a new way of viewing others, a deeper way of comprehending their nature and background. Let love spread contagiously through your community, inviting all to be fully embraced and loved

19

Lost Virtues

Whose power is stronger
Whose generosity more abundant ...
Whose courtesy more gracious.

—Early Docs., 35

As we weave our way through relating and living and loving, it is easy to lose sight of that hidden treasure in the other's heart and to see only the perceived deficient places of personality. Our hearts close to the initial grace that we were blessed by, and this love becomes just another place of work and burden. How sad, that something so alive and wondrous can be consumed by unloving judgment.

Comparison and criticism are the enemies of love. They build walls of hardened thoughts, and we enter strange contests counting love-points day by day. Who is more generous? Who is compromising more? We lose connection with the virtues of faith, hope and love. We scar each other's souls, and love begins to die a long, cruel death. Clare was aware of such destructive behavior and endlessly told her sisters to be especially mindful of the thoughts of their hearts. For if the walls of the heart have harsh edges, then we must look more deeply and find our own reflection in the mirror being held up to us. Only then will we have a chance of freeing ourselves from the insidiousness of judgment, and only then will love have an opportunity to be born once more.

We must be careful, Clare wrote, not to command anything of another that will go against the nature of his or her soul. And if we are experiencing difficulty with certain traits or actions in another, we must pray to the Spirit that "a unity of mutual love" (*Early Docs.*, 74) be present, and that patience may be given. Remember, each soul unfolds in her or his own way and time. If you are the one receiving the critical judgment, pray, writes Clare, for the enlightenment of your heart (*Early Docs.*, 72). Seek the truth in your own soul and see how you can grow closer to God. Love those who persecute, blame, and accuse you. Do not accuse them in return. In this way you enter into the same darkness that Christ agreed to encounter here on earth, and you take a step closer to the light of your own Christ consciousness.

We must always have an open heart and be available so that others will feel free to speak to us at any time about anything, writes Clare. In this way, difficulties can be more easily overcome; through their acknowledgment and expression, they often dissolve in and of themselves. When things are spoken in truth, then Truth is present. When things are received in love, then Love is present. The presence and the power of Truth and Love can hold any difficulty with ease, and they become the cradle for the Beatitudes to come into being. That is, the peacemakers, the justice seekers, the pure and gentle of heart (Matt. 5:1-10) will bring the Kingdom of Heaven into creation right now. Clare quotes Paul (cf.1 Cor 3:9; Rom. 16:3), saying that we are co-creators with God (*The Lady*, 50). We are being asked to live and create this heavenly love on earth with the help and guidance of the Spirit.

When love appears to be absent, may we seek this guidance from the Spirit, and may we work *with* God to create the harmony that is intended for us all.

Companion Meditation:
Coming into the breath of your soul, let yourself feel at rest there. Let go of any tensions or worries. Gently become aware of any places where your

heart may have hardened. Let love come and tenderly soften you. Let love come and gently open you. Let yourself come back to the truth and love of your being, and share that generously with your companion.

Community Meditation:
Does your community have a heart? How is this lived and conveyed to all? Coming into the communal breath, open yourselves to feel the very heart of your community. Let yourselves flow into its energy. Feel the substance of this heart and experience it. Let the love of your heart and the heart of your community become one.

20

The Death Stasis

*Who would not dread the treacheries of the enemy
of humanity who, through arrogance of momentary
and deceptive glories, attempts to reduce to nothing
that which is greater than heaven itself?*

—The Lady, 51–52

Albert Camus, in his book *The Rebel* wrote, "Man is the only creature who refuses to be what he is" (22). To get the full impact of this statement, I think we also need to write, "Woman is the only creature who refuses to be what she is." We are constantly dreaming of being something other than what we are. Yet we really are these magnificent human beings, embodying a love both great and mysterious, with the ability to create our lives in each moment. Unfortunately, we spend a lot of time trying to deny this truth. We reduce who we are and live in a death stasis of discontent and fear.

Clare became distraught when she witnessed the denial of love either in herself or in others. Lack of humility, that is, placing ourselves above God, and the subsequent arrogance of thinking we know better, was for Clare the key factor in denial. The unleashed chain of thoughts, decisions, and repercussions from such arrogance, whether held consciously or unconsciously, can erupt into superiority and inferiority, fear and false bravado, self-centeredness and loneliness, to name just a few of the ailments that result when we are left to our own devices. We live and act from a place of separation—from ourselves, from others, and from God. All of our relationships become ruptured as we fold in on ourselves, forgetting that we are made as relational beings, to live in openness with God and others.

In this place of isolation, as we have denied God's image for us, we must create a self-image that we can live by. This is usually plucked from the world's images—corporate, educational, or spiritual—so that we will be accepted and loved. It is interesting to note how hard we work to attain love and acceptance, the very things we already have from God! And how easily we settle for a dim reflection of self when we could allow the divine and human love to come into union in our own selves. If we only knew what we were denying!

So why do we refuse what we so dearly want and what is so readily available to us? Mostly because we make choices based on our painful past and we want to make sure that we do not experience pain again. By turning away from God and attempting to control our life, we believe we can escape this suffering. Meanwhile, the dull pain of not loving, or being loved, lays waste our souls, leaving us lifeless and dissatisfied, existing in the familiarity of longing rather than truly living. Can we not choose to experience something other? Of course we can, but there is no guarantee of what will come our way.

No wonder Clare was brought to tears as she witnessed people refusing to let the love of God give birth in their bodies and souls, their turning away from the true love giving rise to the very pain they were trying to escape. When we can understand that the true love cannot be grasped or comprehended or even mastered, then we can begin to open to experiences that our human minds cannot even imagine. Herein lies the adventure, and the greatest eternal love affair, with ourselves, with God, and with others. Yes, it is possible!

Companion Meditation:
Drawing into your body and your soul, ask in what areas of your life you turn away from God and away from love. Let them gently speak to you. Lay them tenderly on the breath of love. Release any fear you may feel and

breathe. Know the love you desire is available at every moment. Ask the Spirit to show you how to unfold into this love with yourself and your companion.

Community Meditation:
As a community, do you really open to the Word of God, or do you become preoccupied with a preset agenda and getting things done? Joining together in silence and stillness, allow the spirit of God to come among you. Bring your complete attention to God. Open yourselves to hear the truth and the love wanting to come in. Let your hearts open to the communal love you know is possible.

21

Expectant Lies

Remembering this over and over
leaves my soul sinking within me!

—*The Lady,* 56; cf. Lam. 3:20

One of the surest ways to experience suffering is to live from the lie of expectation. Through the years we create fantasies and ideas regarding our needs and wishes. We then get caught in these falsehoods as our lives may return what we have safely wished for, or we may experience deep disappointment when the needs are not met. We can live from the fear of the unknown, trying to control our lives, or we can abandon ourselves to love and fall into the delicious realm of eternal revelation.

Clare wrote that human beings are full of expectations, secret and otherwise, and they lead us to an erroneous view of God. We set ourselves up for disappointment again and again as we try to figure out the master plan for our lives and demand that it materialize accordingly. As someone said to me, "God does not listen to me." But our deeper souls are constantly guiding us to the truthfulness of the self. All other actions simply reflect our inner fears. We can however, reframe our needs and wishes at any time, choosing to come into a radical faith. If we focus on our fears, then this is where we will live. If we direct our vision to the universal love and support, then it will come running to us.

The way we live with God is the way we live with our companions. What are we demanding from them? How are we keeping them, and ourselves, captive by expecting particular behaviors? Can we have the courage to set them free? These questions open wide the doors to our insecurities, our fears of loss, and our need to control in order to feel safe. We may close our minds and hearts, and say no to the great invitation of life, finding every possible reason to justify our decision. Yet the root of the word *justify* is the same as the root of *justice*, and justice in the biblical understanding is participation in the holiness, that is, wholeness and truthfulness of God. Living in fear is not living in truth, and the truth may be frightening, but freedom of the self is just waiting for us to come and claim ourselves.

Clare and Francis gave each other complete freedom through their love. Their concern was first for their own souls' relationship to God, and then for the other. In this way truth was their language, and love their bed, and they both continually grew into the embodiment of an ever-renewing love. Both had demanding roles to fill in creating a whole new form of community. There was no blueprint for them to follow—they couldn't even follow each other because each of them was initiating something quite different, yet they were able to support each other in the depths and wisdom of love by simply being who they were.

In approximately 1220, Francis went on a missionary journey to Syria. He was gone for so many months that rumors circulated that he had been killed. But then he returned. We can only imagine Clare's soul agony when she thought he may have been dead, but at no time did she try to deter him from his chosen way of life. She kept loving him and loving him, no matter what arose. And with Francis, one certainly needed to expect the unexpected. Such is the way with a person on fire with the passion of truth and love. One never knows where or when God will call, and only those who live without fear will unreservedly follow. Clare and Francis were both followers of an impassioned love that took them through the darkest pain, brought them into the purest light, and transformed their souls, allowing them to love freely. May we have the courage to give up our expectant lies and live in this same way.

Companion Meditation:
Coming into the breath of love, allow yourself to settle deeply into its rhythm. Feel how you are loved. Feel yourself slowly let go of your safety net, and keep breathing in the love. See how you may restrict yourself and your companion through your fears. Gently let these restrictions go, and breathe into the love. Ask for the courage to love freely.

Community Meditation:
In what way is your community restrictive? Where is courage needed to move into more expansive ways of being? Coming together into the breath of the universal Spirit, allow all safety nets to be placed at the feet of God. Let any personal feelings of restriction melt into love. Now open your heart to your community. What do you feel, what do you see? Let the Spirit guide you in love and truth and courage.

Taste: Forbidden Fruit

One word frees us of all the weight
and pain of life: That word is love.

—Sophocles

Dark times are a part of love. If we know this, and prepare ourselves to engage with the darkness, it need not threaten our relationships. Rather, it can be entered and celebrated as we understand that it is taking us further into, and not away from, the depths of love. It is biting deeply into the forbidden fruit of knowledge, creating a new Garden of Eden and a new way of loving.

Throughout this sense, we come face-to-face with our own dark history—sexual and otherwise—and are asked to return to our original integrity of behavior and purity of desire. We are invited to enter into and to taste complete fidelity to self, and to bring this honored being to the world, which awaits us with open and loving arms.

22

Difficult Seeds

*You also know that one who is clothed cannot fight
another who is naked, because she is more quickly
thrown who gives her adversary a chance to get hold
of her.*

—*Early Docs.*, 37

In any relationship, whether it is with God, an intimate partner, or a
friend or colleague, there will come a time of difficulty. Very often
difficulties arise through differing in opinions, or simply not accepting what is being offered to us. Positions are taken, right and wrong
enter the field of play, and individual stubbornness can stop the evolution of understanding. The seeds of discontent begin to germi-
nate—and that is when the real difficulty begins.

Clare was adamant about creating peaceful environments within
her communities. She warned against allowing anger, which only
results in outbursts of temper and separation from love, to overtake
one's disposition. If we become separated from love, she wrote, then
there can be no peace. When we are without peace and love, we are
without God. And when we are without God we find ourselves falling
back into the smallness of our nature, which wants to be right, which
wants to be vindicated at any cost—even to the point of disowning
our peaceful hearts. We are fully clothed and not willing to reveal our
vulnerable nakedness.

Clare teaches that if we find ourselves in a heated disagreement, the remedy does not reside in repeated self-assertion *or* in worry afterwards. She tells us to seek refuge in prayer. We are to ask the person we are having difficulty with to pray for us, that our souls may come back to peace. We are to disrobe from our personal views and grievances, and come back to love and back to God. In this way we invite the other to enter into forgiveness and not into further battle. And where forgiveness is needed, Clare writes, hearts are to be opened, allowing for a divine outpouring of love.

It was well known that Francis's brothers frequently fell into bitter arguments, even though Francis, like Clare, sought the way of peace. Both their teachings were clearly responding to real needs within community life. But what is unknown is that the Franciscan Order is in existence today only thanks to the peacemaking effort and resolve of Clare. After the death of Francis, the male order was in danger of dissolution, as the brothers argued heatedly over the interpretation of their founder's teachings. It was Clare who firmly brought them back to their initial spirit of love, peace, and reliance on God.

In Clare's own life, her calm and loving disposition was constantly reiterated. I wonder, though, how she felt when she asked for Francis to visit her at San Damiano and he declined? In these times of denial, did Clare feel hurt or anger? Were these times sowing difficult seeds for her? We can only assume that her human and womanly self felt various degrees of these emotions, as she makes clear that it was indeed hard for her to be parted for too long from Francis. What personality death did she experience in the process?

Nan C. Merrill's beautiful reinterpretation of Psalm 37 reads, "Recognize your own anger as unfulfilled desire, and lift your thoughts to higher planes." It seems Clare was able to do just this—to use these difficult times to elevate her consciousness to a higher level of loving. By coming into the depth of prayer, by joining with her inner God, she was able to transcend the humanly difficult times and come into a greater selflessness of being and love. She did not turn aside from Francis but instead turned ever more deeply to love. May we learn from her life, and surrender ourselves to the greater love.

Companion Meditation:
If a rift has occurred or a heated argument is in progress between you and your companion, let each retreat from his or her view and come into the breath. Let there be silence and breath only. When both of you are in a place of calm, let there be a spoken intention of returning to the love, and simply sit in this love, with nothing to be done or said. Let love pour through your heart, mind, and fullness of body. When ready, let love speak. Where needed, let love forgive.
(If you are alone, you may use this meditation if old love rifts still live within and need love and forgiveness, or if in a difficulty with a friend).

Community Meditation:
When encountering difficult seeds, let the community gather with the intent of sitting in love, of loving the difficulty itself. Let any notion of fixing, making right, or getting rid of be placed aside. Sigh into the communal love, knowing that this difficulty is given to us all—knowing that it is God coming to meet us. How are we to greet such a God? Open your hearts and let love answer.

23

The Desirous Self

As you further contemplate His ineffable delights,
eternal riches and honors, and sigh for them in the great desire and love of
your heart, may you cry out.

—***Early Docs.,*** *49*

Desire emerges from our deepest being. In the Indian creation myth, as told in the Rig Veda, desire was the first to arise from the dark waters in the beginning of time; it was the bond between being and not-being, giving birth to the rest of creation. The Sufis say that God desired to give expression and form to love, and so created humankind; in such a way we humans have been desiring to know this original love ever since. In the Jewish creation myth, there is the desire of the Creator for an abundant, life-giving earth and the harmonious relationship with, and between, man and woman. Desire and love are intimately entwined in the dark cosmic waters of our souls, yearning for each other through our very life. Clare understood this yearning to be the vehicle for understanding and coming into our true nature of love.

All human beings desire to be happy. We hunger for an absolute happiness that will profoundly engage us in life and love. This engagement, we intuit, goes beyond a temporal and ephemeral satisfaction, and embodies an eternal and sacred quality. Too often, however, our desires for happiness become distorted. We may have the greatest intention for experiencing sacred love, but our loneliness and sense of isolation can draw, or push, us into situations that are not the best for our souls. This distortion can be experienced whether we are in partnership or single.

Our behavior, caused by a perceived lack of love, can cleverly masquerade as coming from our deepest desire for connection and happiness. We can then rationalize our actions as following our truth. More often than not, it is our loneliness that is causing us to act, and it will only be a matter of time before frustration reemerges and the quest begins again. Herein we have the common "love affair," which burns oh so brightly, and oh so quickly, as each seeks to find happiness in the other. Such an attraction can be especially tempting when we are experiencing those "difficult seeds" with our companion and so look elsewhere for love.

Very soon, however, it becomes apparent that no one can provide our happiness. What we are seeking is solely within our own sacred power. The key here is to discern which self is doing the desiring. Is it the smaller self, who cannot see that it lives within the waters of love and therefore seeks itself everywhere on the outside? Or is it the deeper desirous self, consciously seeing itself reflected in another, yet knowing that the greatest love story lives within?

When we are deeply connecting to our inner being of love, we can consciously follow its promptings, knowing that every yearning, every desire, will be bringing it closer to its inner home. If we are merely escaping through denial, or through refusal to reflect honestly, we will find ourselves in a repeated painful and conflicting situation, and we will once more feel the need to seek another. The mature soul patiently watches its own reactions and responses, seeking clarity before it takes action. Only when it feels the calm of the deeper self does it move towards its inner promptings. The immature soul, by contrast, will dive in at the first sign of attraction, creating more soul wounds for both the self and the other.

Clare's words at the opening of this chapter, "As you further contemplate His ineffable delights," clearly indicate the need for taking time to enter into the silence of contemplation when one is struck with desire. She knew desire well, both for God and for Francis. Her self-discipline is to be commended as she acted in accordance with her spirit and not her emotional body. In this way, true love was able to grow within her soul. May we pray for that discipline and for the ability to wait in the silence for God's desire to be revealed.

Companion Meditation:
Come into your place of quiet, and gently breathe into your soul. Allow all desires to emerge, without judgment or denial. Keep breathing into the depth of your soul, and breathe deeply into the love within. Allow the desires to rest in this love. Ask for the clarity of vision to see the truth of these desires. And ask that you may come into appropriate action (or not) as required.

Community Meditation:
What does your community most desire? Sometimes communities become fragmented when too many desires are trying to be instituted. Let this be a meditation on the Unity of Desire. Come together with this intention, and breathe into the spirit of community desire. Allow your souls to be stirred. Allow your true feelings for community to surface without judgment. Deny nothing, and let the Spirit guide you. When ready, give a loving voice to what emerged.

24

The Virginal Return

*[You] are beautifully adorned with the banners
of an undefiled virginity.*

—*The Lady,* 44–45

Sexuality has, for too long, been fraught with casual and abusive qualities. We have not honored our sexual selves, and we have acted with ignorant indiscretion, most often in the hope of finding an elusive love and intimacy. It is time to return to the sacredness of this gift of our sexuality, and to allow it to become what it truly is—a sanctified expression of human love and a powerful way to enter more deeply into the mysteries of our divine self.

Jane Schaberg in *The Illegitimacy of Jesus*, redefines the word *virgin* as "a woman never subdued; a woman who is undefeated, integral, and creative, one who is not identified or destroyed by her relationship with men" (198). We need to read the same for a man; that he is not defeated or destroyed by his relationship with women and that his creative and integral self is developed. If we approach the virginal from a spiritual and psychological perspective, rather than as mere biological fact, we broaden our understanding of the impact it can have on our lives. The virginal return is coming back to one's wholeness or as Schaberg states, "the integral," which comes from the Latin derivative *integer*, meaning untouched or whole. It is not a reclaiming of innocence but rather a returning to our inner place of wisdom and love, the place that is untouched by our earthly experiences, the place that can heal our sexual self-abuse and abuse by others.

Clare writes about the internal dwelling place: "As the glorious virgin of virgins carried [Him] materially, so you, too, by following in her footprints … can, without any doubt, always carry Him spiritually in your chaste and virginal body, holding Him by Whom you and all things are held together" (*The Lady,* 52). By coming into this internal embrace with the Christ love, we can hold all things together, that is, we can take our painful history and hold it in the internal, and eternal, love. Pain and love can live side by side, and slowly the love returns the soul to its original state of being, love, and trust. Any places within the soul that have been put aside or fragmented can come home, back to the loving self. This is the beginning of entering into the mature self. Clare understood this process as she wrote, "In embracing [Him], you are a virgin" (*The Lady,* 44). That is, by embracing the love, you become healed. You become a wholly integrated, creative being who is enhanced and not diminished by relationship.

Clare and Francis, even with their physical separation, held each other in the divine embrace, bringing each other's souls further, and deeper, into the light of love. There was a security in this real love, a deep knowing by their souls of the journey of togetherness and wholeness. They became witnesses to each other of the healing nature of love and gently placed balms of healing kindness upon each other's hearts. May we learn to do the same, helping each other to heal our past sexual wounds and to open once more to our virginal beings of love. We are all called to return. May our world return to the sacredness of our sexuality, placing it high on the altar of love, and, through it, dive deeply into our divine origins.

Companion Meditation:
Create a sacred space for you and your companion to come together (or your own sacred space if alone). Breathe deeply into love. Breathe deeply into your sexual being and your sexual body. Know that you are safe and

held in love. Allow any past hurts or feelings to arise, and give them over to the Christ love. Know that you do not need to repeat these events—they are past. You are here now, and you can create the sexual fulfillment that you desire. Create a safe place to communicate these desires at will.

Please Note: If images arising cause undue stress or anxiety please seek professional guidance and help.

Community Meditation:
This is a meditation for returning to the integral nature of wholeness for your community. Gather together in love, and let go all your notions of what community is. Come into a space of quiet and stillness. When ready, all gently repeat the word community as a mantra, over and over, until you fall into a natural silence. Take note of what images, thoughts, or words were revealed to you. Open the space for sharing these revelations.

25

The Dark Shadow of Love

*Who would not dread the treacheries of the enemy of
humanity who, through the arrogance of momentary and
deceptive glories, attempts to reduce to nothing that which
is greater than heaven itself?*

—***The Lady,*** 51–52

As we move deeper into our selves, and into our partnerships, we are
also brought into the darkness of our souls—the experience of the
cross as a living reality. Carl Jung described the cross as representing
the polarities of opposites, that is, our earthly notions of good and
evil, right and wrong, light and dark. He understood Christ as uniting
these opposites through the power of love, as his divinely destined life
was juxtaposed with a gruesome, and ostensibly useless death. Essentially, Jung was postulating that there is a love beyond all our judgments of a good or bad experience.

To be brought into the darkness of our souls is a gift. It is a gift of
purifying love, in which we come face-to-face with our fears, our
shame, our guilt—anything that keeps us separate from knowing our
own love and the greater love of God. There can be pain as we are
shown past experiences that we would prefer not to revisit, but in
coming into the love of Christ, the one who illumines "those who sit
in darkness and in the shadow of death" (Luke 1:79), we can more
easily let these experiences pass through us and lay them to rest.

Christ said, "resist no evil" (Matt. 5:39), that is, resist nothing that is being brought into your consciousness. It is in the resistance that even more pain is created.

A particularly vulnerable time for women is just before, and during, their menses. Anger, irritation, physical discomfort, and dark moods are common. This is a valuable time for women to encounter the darkness within the soul; it is the soul rising into greater awareness. Paul wrote, "Anything shown up by the light will be illuminated and anything illuminated is itself a light" (NJ Ephesians 5:13–14). That is, the very darkness is the light—an ongoing unification of the opposites within. If one is able to be aware of this process, the menses can be a rich time to bring the soul into greater alignment with the truth of the self.

Men also are given this gift through confrontation, conflict, depression, or any other means the Spirit desires to use. What is important for both women and men is that they pay attention to these soul-stirrings, not projecting them onto others or denying them or busying the self to avoid them, but sitting with them and allowing the Great Love to hold them. We are not required to do anything, as Paul discovered when praying for relief; he was told, "My grace is sufficient for you, for My strength is made perfect in weakness" (2 Cor. 12:9).

Clare gave herself completely to this light of love. It is written about her, "O how great is the vibrancy of this light and how intense is the brilliance of its illumination!" (*The Lady*, 264). She took everything to Christ. In return, Christ gave her everything: the dark and the light, the good and the bad, the shadow and the brightness. Her soul was raised in and through these opposites to the unification in love. Her lack of resistance to all that was given was her savior. She did not blame Francis, or others, for anything. She stood up in her weakness and in the darkness, and let her soul be purified. She would, I am sure, agree with Rumi, as he wrote, "You are so weak. Give up to Grace" (25).

If we do not give ourselves up to this grace, if we refuse to sit in the darkness, we become lost lovers of God. Our hearts constrict, and our intimacy with our companions and community loses its vibrancy. May we have the courage and wisdom to know that the Great Love is everything, and everywhere, even in the darkest of shadows.

Companion Meditation:
Bring yourself to sit in love. Let the light within shine. Let the gift of darkness come to visit if it desires. Do not be afraid, you are held in love. You are love. Bless the messenger and what it brings you. Lay it upon the heart of Christ. Withdraw any projections onto your companion. Bless them with love, and open once more to an intimate love, with both yourself and your companion.

Community Meditation:
We have not only personal darkness but also a collective darkness. What is the darkness of your community? Bring yourselves into the light of love and let it surround the whole community. Gently open the community circle to allow any darkness that the Spirit wants to be seen. Hold it tenderly in love. Bless it and let it go back into the light. When you are ready, share any insights that have come to you during the meditation.

26

Hidden Sweetness

*So that you too may feel what friends feel in
tasting the hidden sweetness that, from the
beginning, God Himself has reserved for His
lovers.*

—***The Lady,** 51*

We are all gentle beings with an inherent sweetness waiting to be
lived. Our world needs these wonderful human qualities, and so do
our souls. Jesus said, "Learn from me, for I am gentle and humble in
heart" (NJ Matt. 11:29). Claire Marie Ledoux, in *Clare of Assisi: Her
Spirituality Revealed in Her Letters*, writes, "The Jesus who is saying
this is the supreme revelation of the sweetness of God" (66). We also
are these sweet revelations.

In first encountering our companions, we are often given a glimpse
of the 'hidden sweetness' of their souls. Love gathers us together, and
we swim in a seemingly endless ocean of love and possibilities. Then,
at some point, the obscuration occurs. One or both people no longer
feel or see the ocean of love. Judgment, accusation, and those dark
shadows threaten the very life of love. Without conscious recognition
of this occurrence, love can fall away and only absence and discontent
remain.

What is required is the commitment to be witnesses for each other
of the Great Love that lives within. When one person has fallen away

from this knowledge, it is vital that the other continue to see their companion's hidden divine soul and hold that vision until the companion can return to his or her truth. In such a way, we are being a container of love for our companion's wounded self. This holding does not require that we do anything or try to fix anything; we merely sit and hold our companion's soul in the divine love. Humans can only resist love for so long, and with the grace of God, our companion will return.

If, when our companion has turned aside from love, we take it as a personal turning away from us, then the automatic reaction is to turn away as well. But in doing so, we are retreating from our own inner love, and we create a false and harmful situation for ourselves and our companion. This can escalate to dire misunderstandings and sometimes the end of a relationship. Rumi writes, *"Look as long as you can at the friend you love, no matter whether that friend is moving away from you or coming back toward you"* (26). In such a way we also take responsibility for our own knowledge of being loved. We do not rely on another to confirm the truth that we are loved and lovable.

Clare and Francis ably held each other's souls in the vision of the hidden sweetness. Clare, in particular, was the source of light for Francis when he encountered times of darkness, pain, and confusion. He sought her presence, knowing she could hold his soul, and his body, in the radiant light of love. Did she ever let go of this vision? I think not. This is the true sacred companionship; knowing that we are always held in love, no matter what the state of our soul or what we are experiencing.

When both partners lose sight of their love, much harm can occur. Clare writes, "May neither bitterness nor a cloud overwhelm you" (*The Lady*, 51). If you feel this bitterness creeping into your soul, in relation to either yourself or your companion, immediately seek your place once more in love. Do not let any disdain become rigidified in your soul, but rather know that all obstacles are callings to enter ever more deeply into love. They are not the messengers of the death of a relationship; they are ways to enter into a renewal of love, again and again. Let each of us be responsible and accountable in the challenge of this renewal, and may we help one another to remove the veils from our souls, so that we can become those gentle and sweet revelations of God. Paul wrote, "But we all, with unveiled faces, beholding as in a mirror the glory of the Lord, are being transformed into the same image from glory to glory." (2 Cor. 3:18). May we be this mirror of God for one another.

Companion Meditation:
Bring yourself into the place of quiet. Allow yourself to lower gently into the hidden sweetness of your soul. Sit here and breathe and taste this sweetness. Know this to be your true home. Notice any thoughts or feelings that may arise. See how you may turn aside from your innate gentleness. See how you may turn away from your companion. Come back to the sweetness, and hold yourself and your companion in this vision of love.

Community Meditation:
How does sweetness enter into your community tasks and responsibilities? Let this be a meditation of Active Sweetness. Come together in the spirit of the sweet and humble heart. Allow this spirit to enter into the depths of the heart and soul of your community and one another. See how your work may be infused with sweetness. Breathe into this place and open your soul to receive its grace.

27

The Infatuation

*"All you who pass by the way, look and see
if there is any suffering like my suffering!"*

—The Lady, 56

Infatuation is the dark side of desire. Seduction is its eldest brother, and both lure one away from the inner foundation of self. Seduction is nothing more than illusion, because it is based not on an equal meeting in love but a leaving of self to be entrapped by another. Infatuation quickly follows, as having left the self, the soul needs to seek its own beauty and love in another. This pursuit can only lead to suffering, and the illusory notion that one is entering into love. Andreas Capellanus writes, "Love is a certain inborn suffering derived from the sight and excessive meditation upon the beauty of the opposite sex" (28). In fact, this is not the truth of love but an immature infatuation.

If we enter into an infatuated relationship, we forgo our power of choice and our own inner power. We allow ourselves to both possess and be possessed, and the emotions become the foundation for our relating. This is where the suffering is paramount. Jealousy can rip the heart open, and even the slightest turning away of our lover can cause anguish and intense sadness. We become slaves to a false love rather than attaining the freedom of the real love that is available to us.

It is written in the Gospel of Philip, "When immature women see a man sitting alone, they go to him, flirt with him, and distract him. Likewise, when immature men see a pretty woman sitting alone, they hunger for her, seduce her, and she lets herself be taken" (89). Flirtation unfortunately has become a common method of communication. It is nothing more than ignorance of how to honor oneself and another. Those who have "the Holy Breath in them," however, are "free of the world [and] can no longer be made into a slave there" (*Gospel of Philip*, 91). That is, by living from our sacredness, we will no longer fall prey to the illusory and momentary attractions. Real attraction and real love, which is ultimately what we all desire, then has a chance.

Sexual maturity and an honoring of its sacredness are essential for community living; without them, emotional and spiritual bedlam can ensue, as has been made clearly evident in all kinds of communities—political, spiritual, family, and work—by way of illicit affairs, pedophilia, and sexual harassment. Desire can quickly grow into a darkness that no human being should have to endure, either as perpetrator or as victim. This darkness is a profound degradation of a spiritually magnificent gift, which is ultimately designed to bring us closer to God and to each other. We need to rescue the desire for real love and its expression, by bringing our nature into its utmost integrity and impeccability.

Clare was well known for her integrity, and it is written that she walked in "the footprint of the Mother" (*The Lady*, 279), that is, her nature embodied the purity of the Word, just as Mary's body contained Jesus. Clare lived in genuine purity, gaining freedom from the many seductions of the world.

It is essential for the leaders of our communities not to be seduced, either by personal attraction, or by promises of wealth and power. And it is important to acknowledge that we *all* have the responsibility to live in freedom from seduction and infatuation. In the words of Mahatma Ghandi, "We need to be the change we wish to see."

Companion Meditation:
Bring yourself into a place of deep quiet and stillness. Breathe into love and the freedom of self. Take time to rest here. Then allow for a gentle rising of any ways that you are not free. See what seductions, what infatuations, keep you bound. Bring them tenderly into the sacred love of the Mother. Ask that your soul may know its sacredness, and see you honoring your self, your companion, and all beings.

Community Meditation:
Every community falls prey to infatuation and seduction. What began as a vision can turn into an obsessive desire, and there can be seduction in reaching goals through means not filled with integrity. Let this be a meditation of Returning to Purity. Gathering in silence, let the purity of Mother Mary come to guide you. Place yourselves in her mantle of caring love. Let your minds and hearts be washed clean. Open to receive the guidance for each, personally and collectively. Share what you have received.

28

Total Fidelity

*And, after all who ensnare their blind lovers
in a deceitful and turbulent world have been
completely passed over, may you totally love Him.*

—*The Lady,* 51

The word *fidelity,* meaning faithfulness and loyalty, is mostly used in association with another person. It is also defined, however, as "conformity to truth" (*Concise Oxford Dictionary*). Taking this definition, we come closer to Clare's understanding: a total faithfulness to love, which is ultimately found in the deep inner self. She writes of being taken into the "heavenly bridal chamber," and the commitment made therein to the God of love, the God of union. Be mindful, she says, of "believing nothing, agreeing with nothing that would dissuade you from this commitment"(*The Lady,* 47–48).

When we are drawn into companionships, it is of great importance to understand what is creating the feeling of union. Our souls are led to others to see our own reflections, both the human wounding and the divine splendor. If we join through the wounding only, we enter into a sympathetic union but also develop a codependency as we seek to soothe our souls over and over in the other, with no real transformation. If we pass over the human self and join only in the divine essence, we are living in denial and separate ourselves from the all-accepting and encompassing love. The real union of love joins both our human and divine aspects with our own selves and with another.

Jesus wept when he heard of the death of his friend Lazarus. Through this weeping he honored his human emotional self, staying in the tomb long enough to humanly mourn. But then he entered into the transcendent nature of love and raised Lazarus once more to life (John 11:35–44). Are we able to weep for ourselves and then be raised into the transcendence of love? Are we able to feel another's pain and then see the transcendent nature of love that holds him or her? This is true fidelity to the self, and to the God of love.

Claire Marie Ledoux, writes, "There is this tragic conflict between what we are and what we do and, at the same time, a constant progress when we become our own masters, a progress that is built up in terms of humanization. Self-control enables us to go to God along our most personal paths and by achieving our own freedom" (73). Coming to know our deeper selves demands that our behaviors change accordingly. What was an appropriate action previously is no longer truthful; we need to learn to honor the growth of our souls. In times of transition, self-control is necessary; these are times of learning to know who we are and those who join us on our journey.

Freedom is what we all ultimately seek, and Clare teaches us how to come into its presence. She did not have any hidden agendas or vested interests with Francis, or with her community. This is a beautiful example of self-control, that is, not attempting to control her external environment. Clare was completely faithful to and trusted the love of God that lived within her. She also trusted herself and her commitment to the spirit of love, coming freely into the nakedness of her own soul.

As she prepared to pass from this life, it was recorded that Clare was saying "there was nothing to fear," and that "she would be safe and taken care of." When asked as to whom she was speaking, she replied, "My soul." She did not attempt to hide her fears. Nor did she conceal her feelings for Francis. Their companionship was well known within her community. This was her fidelity to self, to truth, and to her love for her companion.

May we find the way to be faithful to ourselves and to others. For too long we have been hiding from our truth, keeping our innate treasure locked away from the world. Rumi writes, *"Love wants a lover"* (22). It is time to commit once more to this love, and to share all that we are. The world needs us. We need us.

Companion Meditation:
Come to your meditation with the intent of blessing yourself with love. Slowly breathe into this love. Breathe into the truth of your own soul. See how you are unfaithful to yourself. See how you are unfaithful to your companion. Recommit to your own love. Recommit to your companion.

Community Meditation:
How are you unfaithful to yourself and your community? Let this be a meditation of Faithfulness to Truth. Come together, knowing that you are all loved just as you are. Breathe into this love that is holding you. Breathe into the love that is within you. Let it show you how you may bring forward your treasure to share with all. Recommit to sharing who you are. Recommit to your community love.

Touch: The Original Embrace

I merely stir, press, feel with my fingers,
and am happy. To touch my person to some one
else's is about as much as I can stand.

—Walt Whitman

Our bodies are not merely gifts—they are the divine incarnated. We are the divine incarnated, and our human bodies and the human touch can help awaken this knowledge within us.

In this sense we move into the physical expression of love and learn how we can reclaim the sacredness of our sexuality. For too long we have misused our bodies in an attempt to find intimacy and to feel loved. We are now being asked to begin anew with our sexual expression, and to slowly enter into the Holy of Holies, the divine sanctuary within, with the respect and honor that we all deserve.

29

Eternal Moment

What a great and praiseworthy exchange:
to leave the things of time for those
of eternity.

—***Early Docs.****, 37*

The eternal moment is now. There are two ways we can live in this life of eternity: we can enter into brief and fleeting encounters with others, moving through time in an apparently spontaneous manner but with little or no accountability for our actions; or we can enter into the breadth and depth of our soul relations, with both self and others, coming into a stability that is at once grounded in this human reality and, simultaneously, living in the eternal fullness of the moment. Clare was an adept at the latter.

The original community of sisters often experienced times when the larder was running close to bare, and they would fret about their bodily survival. In one instance there was only a half loaf of bread, and Clare directed a sister to make fifty slices out of it. The incredulous sister began, and indeed she did cut fifty slices (*The Lady,* 170). Another time there was no oil. Clare asked a brother to place the oil jar on the wall of their monastery. When he later returned, the jar was full. We often call such events miracles. I understand them as Clare entering into the absolute fullness of the eternal moment. She did not perceive any lack, and she did not deny the physical need. She simply allowed the physicality of human existence to become one with the ever-present eternity. This conjoining of realities is everyone's responsibility on earth, and it involves all of who we are, that is, our physical, emotional, and spiritual beings.

Jean Pierre de Caussade beautifully describes the "sacrament of the present moment" as "ceasing to thread this day to the painful past or relating it to a frightening future." All of the troubles within our mind and heart arise when we are relating our present-day living to either the past or the future; in doing so we are not living in the sacramental moment. Unlike Clare, we have lost our connection to that eternal fullness and are busy reliving old moments again and again. This is especially so in our relationships. Love has so many painful associations, and by living from them, we limit what we can experience and where we can travel in the glorious eternity available to us.

There is only one way to come into the radiant present, and that is to feel all that we did not feel in the past. If we have emotions that were not expressed at the time they were felt, they remain alive and await our attention. This may seem like a frightening and arduous task, but all they are asking is to be heard, and we quickly learn that this is a very liberating process. Unshed tears are finally released, cleansing the heart of its painful wounds, so that we may sing with the Psalmist, "Create in me a clean heart, O Gracious One, and put a new and right spirit within me. Enfold me in the arms of love, and fill me with your Holy Spirit." (Nan Merrill, Psalm 51). With this new heart and renewed spirit we can learn to love again in the eternal moment.

As we begin to live in this love, we must continue to honor our emotional expression, as best we can, in the very moment of the experience. Through this expression we are loving and honoring our selves in the most beautiful and simple way. This self-loving is needed for our soul development, and essential before we bring our bodies into the lovemaking process. In this way, our hearts remain clear and able to fully encounter love in the present. This is the fundamental sacrament of love. May we all come into our heart feelings and give ourselves time to bring them into the light of love.

Companion Meditation:
You may choose to do this meditation alone, or you may wish the support
of your companion, simply sitting with you and holding the space of love
for you. Your companion is not there to take away or even soothe your
experience—he or she is simply there to hold you in love and allow you to
feel all you need to feel.

Come and breathe into the quiet of your soul. Feel yourself in the fullness
of love. Let yourself be held here. Then slowly allow the feelings of your
heart to arise. Do not push them away. Do not hold on to them. Simply
let them come in and through you, allowing them the freedom to express
how they desire. Know you are held in love throughout—there is nothing
to fear. Allow the tears to flow, the heart to be cleansed, and your spirit to
be renewed in the eternal love.

Community Meditation:
Let this be a Heart-Cleansing Meditation for your community. It is easy
for the heart of a community to become closed when emotions are not
expressed. Join together in love, with the intention of both a personal and
a community cleansing. Breathe deeply into your own heart and the larger
community heart. Let these hearts open to you. Breathe into love. Allow
whatever feelings come to arise. Love them gently, and let tears flow. Let
all hearts be cleansed together in the eternal love, once more uniting in the
Heart of God.

30

God's Body

She broke open the alabaster jar of her body ... so that the house of the Church would be filled with the fragrance of her ointments.

—*The Lady,* 288

The human body is the living sacrament of the divine presence. There is a dire need to return the body to its rightful and respected place in our world. Christianity has destroyed our relationship with our bodies, historically moving from fear of the body, through denial and neglect, and currently sitting at indifference. It is vital that we stop casting the body aside as something other than God. We need to see it for what it is—a miracle of life that deserves to be honored with our soul and spirit.

Clare wrote, "Through contemplation, transform your entire being into the image of the Godhead Itself" (*The Lady,* 51). Her writings consistently marvel at the nature of the human body, which she understood to clothe our God, and who, through the body, enters into the heart of human matter. It is given to us human beings to come into right relationship with this divine essence presenting itself in the form of our bodies. In the Gospel of Philip it is written, "Do not fear nor be enamored of it. If you fear it, it will rule you. If you love it, it will paralyze you and devour you" (93). That is, we are neither to deny the body nor to become obsessed with its condition or pleasures, whether sexually or in relation to its health and appearance.

We are to treat both our own bodies and the bodies of others with complete respect and honor. Our sexual lives need to reenter the sacred dimension, where we find the hallowed echo of Genesis 2:25, "And they were both naked, the man and his wife, and were not ashamed." We need to relearn what it is to be with one another in complete honesty and nakedness, laying aside our personal wants and needs, and instead seeing our bodily joining as a spiritual prayer, bringing us closer to the experience of the Godhead. In *The Alchemy of Desire*, Tarun Tejpal writes, "The truth is, godhead is tangible" (4). There is no greater experience of this tangibility than through the commingling of our energy and bodies.

Paul, in Romans 12:1–2 (NJ), writes, "present your bodies as a living sacrifice, dedicated … to God", and that we are not to conform to this world, "but let the renewing of your minds transform you." What a beautifully full command. He is asking us to move beyond the worldly conceptions of the body, and to bring our minds and bodies before God to be transformed. Returning to Clare's message, "through contemplation, transform your entire being," we see that she is inviting us to come back to the Great Silence within our souls. This is where the transformation occurs.

It is through this silence that we are brought into an awareness of our unified existence, which includes the body and all that we are. This is how our bodies can return to their original holiness of being. Come into the silence, and take your time getting to know your own body. Take your time getting to know the body of your companion. Sit with the tangibility of God, first within yourself, and then with the other. Do not be in a hurry. We have for too long been divorced from our sacred sexual nature, and we need time to reintegrate all those elements that have kept us apart from our sacred selves. "May the God of peace Himself sanctify you completely; and may your whole spirit, soul, and body be preserved blameless." (1 Thess. 5:23).

Meditation: (To be done alone)
Lie down comfortably on the floor. Bring your awareness to all the parts of your body touching the floor, and breathe deeply. Find your own natural rhythm of breathing, and consciously breathe into every part of your body. Slowly allow yourself to settle into the quiet stillness of the center of your being. Breathe from here. Feel your body as if for the first time. Let it gently stretch if it wishes. Let this be an exploration. Bless your body with love.

Companion Meditation: (To be done together)
Lie down with your companion, side by side, with arms and legs gently touching. Come into your own breath, and let that breath move through the whole of your body. Come into your quiet, still center. Feel the very foundation of yourself and breathe from here. As you feel ready, expand your awareness to your companion, becoming aware of her energy, of his breath, not doing anything, but simply opening to an expansiveness of your being and your companion's together. When you are ready, bring your awareness back to yourself.

Community Meditation:
Let this be a meditation of Transforming the Mind of the Community. Gather with the intention of transforming old thought patterns, both personally and collectively. Come together in the spirit of love and truth. Breathe deeply into the stillness of your being. Pay attention to what forms arise for you. Discern if they are of a personal or a community nature. Let the transformation occur—not through doing anything but simply by allowing the spirit of love to renew as it desires.

31

Enlightened Love

*The most high heavenly Father saw fit
in mercy and grace to enlighten my heart.*

—*The Lady*, 61

Clare's enlightened state of being was becoming well known in Italy and other parts of Europe long before she died. Her life became a model for many women, and there is much evidence that she was held in the utmost respect and reverence by male counterparts as well. This included the Popes, who visited her at San Damiano because they recognized her sanctity and sought her blessings and spiritual advice.

Clare's soul was able to activate healing and wholeness in others. There are many documented accounts of this ability, both while she was alive and after her death. Living from the pureness of her being allowed the healing love to radiate from her heart, awakening the inherent love in another. Francis knew this well and availed himself of the feminine radiance flowing through Clare. He knew that she embraced the divine female mysteries, and he honored these (and at times feared them). He acknowledged that Clare could assist him in accessing his own mysteries in a way he was unable to do alone. She also recognized this gift that Francis brought her. This knowledge allowed both of them to enter more deeply into their sacred selves. This is the archetype of the sacred companion, bringing the feminine and the masculine, and the human and the divine, into a sacred inter-dependence.

Today we have replaced interdependence with independence. Swinging from the pendulum of attachment to the misplaced strength of independence, we have lost our way in the world of relationship. Women have lost the connection with their feminine power and mystery, or if they do access it, it is often misused as a power over another rather than as an offering of the true self. Men crumble under this misuse of feminine energy, and either find themselves in an accusatory and controlling situation or run for their lives. It is time to learn once more how to enter into the divine mysteries of relationship, offering ourselves to one another in a wholesome, enlightened way that will allow for the true communion of two beings.

Women need to return to their bodies and to access the mystery within. There is a divine sense of self waiting to be activated through the physical body. This is the truth of our spiritual and material unification on this earth. Once this mystery is entered, it needs to be shared lovingly, allowing the man to step beside the woman and then the two to enter into the divine gift together. It is not for the woman to be the sole keeper of the mystery, and it is not for the man to enter this territory without self-responsibility—this promotes codependency. Rather, activation of the heart and soul occurs through the feminine invitation and then is responded to by the masculine energy coming to wholly meet and join her.

In the Eastern religions, the tantric teachings embody both feminine and masculine energies. The female is the active principle and the male is the passive, and it is taught that their union can be experienced through the sacred sexual act. *Tantric* means to expand and to weave. It is an expansion of consciousness and a weaving of the energies to bring one closer to the experience of God or enlightenment. Tantra is perceived as one of the most powerful means to encounter the Godhead within our own souls and within another.

In the West we have a long way to go before we can fully grasp the power contained in these mysteries, but an awakening is beginning to happen. As with any divine mystery, it is best to let our souls slowly unfold into it, so that our consciousness can fully absorb and integrate this mystery in a healthy way, and not be shocked into a new form of being that leaves the soul in confusion and fear. Let the gentleness and enlightened heart of Clare guide you in your explorations.

Meditation:(To be done alone)
For the Female: Breathe deeply into your feminine self. Let yourself be taken into the mystery of what it means to be a woman. Bathe there. Swim there. Immerse yourself in the divine feminine mystery. Know this is who you are.

For the Male: Breathe deeply into your masculine self. Feel what it is to be the divine masculine energy. Connect to the very source of this energy. Breathe here and feel yourself grounded in the divine masculine. Honor who you are.

Companion Meditation:
Coming together, sit close, facing each other. Make a physical connection, through holding hands, placing hands on each other's heart center, or whatever feels comfortable for you both. Begin by breathing into your own feminine energy (for the woman) and masculine energy (for the man). (Those in a same-sex union may choose either the male or the female energy.) When you are feeling comfortably grounded in this energy, indicate to your companion (through a gentle squeeze of the hand or slightly more pressure on the palm), and allow the energies to begin circulating to each other—breathing out your feminine energy and breathing in the masculine energy and vice versa. Let this exchange be gentle and loving. When you feel a natural completion, again indicate to your companion, and return to your own energy and natural breath. You may choose to do this meditation with eyes open or closed.

Community Meditation:
Is your community in a state of balance? Is there excessive female energy, or excessive male energy? Let this meditation be one of Right Balance. Even if members of one sex outnumber the other, you can bring the community into balance with your energy. Come together, and first breathe into your feminine energy (both women and men). Feel what this means for you as a community. See how it is important. See where it may be imbalanced. Then breathe into your masculine energy (both men and women). Again, let the vision of its importance rise, and see any place of imbalance. Ask the Spirit to show you the way to bring the community into a feminine and masculine equality.

32

The Kiss of God

Your left hand is under my head and
your right hand will embrace me happily,
You will kiss me with the happiest kiss of
Your mouth.

—*The Lady*, 57

Clare often reflected upon this quotation from the Song of Songs. It seems both to have epitomized for her the tender and supporting nature of her God-lover and to have been the portal into a trusting and divine communion. In allowing oneself to sink deeply into these poetic words, one abandons both body and soul into a consciousness of love and grace. How often do we really allow ourselves to feel, and enter into, such a complete and loving embrace, to be truly held by God or by another? And what is this divine kiss that opens the door of the soul?

In the Hebrew language, the word for *kiss (nashak)* means "to share the same breath," "to breathe together." And the word for *breath* is the same as that for *spirit (ruach)*. In entering into a kiss, we are uniting one breath with another, one spirit with another. It is a fusing of energies and the preliminary stage of union (Leloup, 87). Too often we treat the kiss as something casual, offering our lips and breath and spirit to another without real consideration of what we are giving or what we are entering into. We act on a momentary impulse of wanting to join with another, but we are now being called to a much more conscious action, a magnification of the love and spirit that reside within.

In the Gospel of Philip, it is written, "The realized human is fertilized by a kiss, and is born through a kiss. This is why we kiss each other, giving birth to each other through the love [*kharis*, also grace] that is in us" (63). Our spirits are demanding that we abandon random acts of unconscious behavior and come into the greater realization of our being. Also, we are being asked to acknowledge that we can help one another do this. In fact, we *need* one another to do this. This is a delightful need of humility and openness. It is not a need of neuroticism to buffer one's self-image or ego needs; it is a basic spiritual need for the realization of our souls. It is a humble walk into our own souls, and into God.

We can only wonder about the depths that Clare and Francis would have reached if their relationship had included the physical expression of their love. Nevertheless, we must acknowledge the depth of their shared love, in and through the Spirit. Their words of love and doubt and joy and fear and sorrow were shared with a sacred breath, opening the way for deeply intimate encounters. By abandoning their souls and bodies to the love of God, which lived so fully within them, they were "giving birth to each other" through the sacred kiss of love and life. We are now being asked to do the same, and even more. We are being asked to surrender ourselves to the greater love within, and the love that exists between our companions and ourselves, on every possible level.

It is often the physical level that creates both the most difficulty and the most wondrous sense of divine intimacy and union. May we reconsider what is occurring through our physical kisses and bring the consciousness of the breath and spirit to our actions. May we honor this breath and spirit, both our own and those of the people we are kissing, and learn to walk humbly in the presence of such grace. And may our bodies gently abandon themselves to the loving embrace of God and one another.

Meditation: (To be done alone)
Come and sit in the quietness of the self. Focus on the breath, simply letting it move in and out of the body. Bring to your awareness that your
breath is the spirit of love. Breathe in this spirit of love. Breathe out this
spirit of love. Gently, allow your whole body to be held by this loving
grace.

Companion Meditation 1:
Coming together, sit close, facing each other. Let each go into his or her
breath, gently feeling it moving through the whole body. Be aware that
this breath moving through you is the very spirit of love and grace. When
both are ready, let a gentle kiss pass between you, breathing the love into
each other. With your lips gently resting together, see if you can synchro-
nize your breathing. As one breathes out, let the other breathe in, and vice
versa, finding a natural rhythm. Keep the intention of breathing the loving spirit to each other. In this way, you are breathing in the loving spirit
of your companion and breathing out your loving spirit in return. Keep
going as long as it is comfortable. Let a loving kiss end this meditation.

Companion Meditation 2:
This is a meditation of the Full Embrace. Choose who is to be held, and
then find a comfortable way of sitting where the companion holding may
bear the full weight of the other. Let the intention be that the one who is
holding be the unconditional loving arms of the Mother/Father God, as
well as his or her own unconditional loving arms. Let the one being held
come into the arms of the loving companion with complete abandon, gently unfolding and slowly releasing the body more and more. Immerse the
whole body and soul into the loving embrace. Keep letting go until the
whole body is released. Stay here as long as needed, and let flow whatever
needs to flow through your soul. (For the fullest benefit of this meditation,
choose a completely separate time/day to reverse roles.)

Community Meditation:
What are you embracing as a community? Let this meditation be an exploration into what is being held on a communal level. Gather and breathe into the spirit of love and grace. Let this breath move through each person individually, and then collectively. Allow the body of each person and the body of the community to lean gently into the loving arms of the Mother/Father God and the divine essence of love. Let the Spirit show you what you are embracing, and what may need to be embraced now.

33

Lover's Delight

When you have loved [Him], You are chaste;
when you have touched [Him], You become more pure;
when you have accepted [Him], You are a virgin.

—***Early Docs.**, 35*

Everybody desires to be touched. Our bodies ache for the expression of love to come and caress them. As we continue our spiritual evolution, we are moving into a new era of loving, and touching, and being touched. It is always a confusing time when new paradigms are making their way into our psyches; we are still identifying with old ways and desires while, simultaneously, our souls are urging us to unknown yet somehow known places of delight. We are all being called to be touched in new ways, through both body and soul.

What was it that Clare and Francis were being deeply touched by, that enabled them to offer their souls in such mysterious abandonment to God and each other? A returning to the simplicity of the Gospel and daily living with lovingkindness certainly created their spiritual foundation, but a deeper union was also occurring. This union was their dedication to the sacred wounds of Christ. This was not a devotion to personal suffering (as the Church has so wrongly interpreted historically) but rather a deep commitment to compassion. It was recognition of the human wounds that are incurred upon this earth, and the need for a healing and compassionate salve.

Clare would pray daily in honor of the Five Wounds, recounting their sacredness and asking for the loving grace of Christ to come to both her soul and her body. The prayer to the Wound in the Side was especially poignant, as she looked to the heart of Christ, which had been revealed through the wound, and gratefully acknowledged that this wounded heart remains open for us so that we might find refuge there (De Robeck, 156). This was Clare's sanctuary, and also that of Francis. Clare taught Francis how to hold himself and his wounds gently, and in their being able to do this together, first for themselves and then for each other, their hearts were immersed in a beautiful healing of the Christ energy. Through this healing, their hearts were opened, and Clare and Francis became for each other the living compassion of Christ. They then took this compassion to their immediate communities, and ultimately, it spread to their sisters and brothers throughout the world.

In the quotation that opens this chapter, Clare speaks of loving, touching, and accepting the Christ within. Anyone who has been authentic to his or her spiritual journey will know that when we allow ourselves to enter into the relationship that Clare is suggesting (with Christ or the divine essence), all within us that is not loved, touched, or accepted will arise to meet us. If, as we experienced in the preceding sense, we are able to meet and greet these heart wounds, then we open the way to delight in our original purity, that is, the virginal essence that remains in love and has known nothing other than love. The human touch is a beautiful pathway to return to this, our first home.

Walt Whitman writes, "Divine am I inside and out, and I make holy whatever I touch or am touched from"(*Leaves of Grass*, 38). This is where our intention is vital. What are we doing when we touch another? Are we seeking something from him or her? Clare is asking us to return to our purity, both in mind and in body, and to bring the compassionate love of Christ into every facet of our living and loving.

We are here to be bearers of love, to lovingly accept and gently touch ourselves and one another, physically, emotionally, and spiritually. This is the journey of the lover's delight. In this way we can let go of the identity that has been created out of past experiences and enter into a whole new way of being, the being that God wants us to be. Walt Whitman so beautifully states this (ibid, 41).,

> *"Is this then a touch? …*
> *Quivering me to a new identity,*
> *Flames and ether making a rush for my veins."*

May we all feel this burning rush of our loving and compassionate selves coming back to the home of delight.

Companion Meditation:
Have the intention of coming together without sexual energy or actions. Let this be a meditation of compassion and love, without demand or need to perform. Come together, in nakedness of both body and soul, lying close to each other with bodies gently touching. Go deeply into your breath, and let it fill your whole body. Let the body completely relax in love. Take your time to be here. When ready, gently begin to stroke or touch your companion where you are intuitively drawn. (You may wish to take turns touching each other, or you may wish to touch each other at the same time. Let your hearts guide you.) Let love guide you, and open your heart to what is needed in the moment. Let tears fall, let delight sing. There is nothing that you should not feel. Be open and honest, and let your sacred wounds be healed by the living waters of love. Receive, and breathe into, the compassionate love of the inner divine essence of both yourself and your companion.
(If alone, follow as above and enter into a gentle self-massage, allowing love and compassion to fill your body and soul).

Community Meditation:
Who is your community being touched by, and who is your community touching? As we form communities, it is very easy to become insular and fail to allow the world to touch us, or to reach out to the world commu-

nity. Come together with an openness of heart, and bring the breath deeply into your body. Let the whole body fully relax. Allow the door of your soul to open, and let it be touched by the divine love. Is there something or somebody in the world that could help your community to become more loving and compassionate? Where in the world are the Sacred Wounds of Christ crying out to be loved? Share your thoughts and visions.

34

Infinite Love-Making

*Until we meet at the throne of the glory
of the great God, and desire [this] for us.*

—***The Lady,*** 58

It is time to return to a sacred eroticism. Our sexuality is based on our needing and wanting another (which is a form of possession), and when that need and desire has been satiated, our sexual lives begin to decline. Rumi understood this well, as he writes,

> *"You say you have no sexual longing any more.
> You're one with the one you love.*
>
> *This is dangerous.
> Don't believe that I have a love like that"* (19)

We need to turn away from the societal norms of sexual desire and seek the throne of God, that is, the Holy of Holies or the divine sanctuary. This sanctified place resides in each of us and when we enter it with reverence, the true sexual union can occur, *and* can keep growing.

Clare and Francis threw away the norms of their society from their first secret meetings. And when Clare went to join Francis, she was literally running away from home in the middle of the night to join a band of men who were known to be "touched by some kind of madness." Francis, by accepting her, ritualistically cutting her hair, and giving her the same robes that he and the brothers wore, was acting as only a bishop was ordained to do. That is, he was accepting her into a new form of life, where her soul and body were "officially" consecrated to God. Even a priest did not have the authority to perform such an act, yet Francis, as a layperson, undertook what he felt called to do. Clare responded without question, as she followed her soul's need and destiny. Neither was bound, or dictated to, by Church or society.

Through these initial actions, Clare and Francis were opening the way for creating new forms of love, with each other and with the communities they would create. After their secret meetings, where they conversed at length, they arrived at the moment of "consecrated action." That is, a coming together in the full understanding and consciousness of joining their lives in a shared desire, with the divine grace leading them into the fullness of being. It was a marriage not to each other but to the same divine quest. Yet their souls were so aligned, with both completely surrendering to love, that it is easy to view their relationship as a marriage of the highest possible nature.

Andreas Capellanus writes, "Since ancient times four separate stages of love have been distinguished. The first stage lies in allowing the suitor hope, the second in granting a kiss, the third in the enjoyment of an embrace, and the fourth is consummated in the yielding of the whole person" (121). Treatises on love and sexual union from ancient and medieval times abound. In them a common motif is the Garden of Love, where lovers separate themselves from the world and its ways, and for a time, create their own paradise. It is a place where lovers recline in the shade of the tree, reading poetry, playing music, and giving over to their hearts' passion. There is an entering into the "Holy of Holies, the bridal chamber, or communion" (Leloup, 107). It is here that souls and bodies lie down in trust and consciousness.

Where does love begin? Where do God and we as lovers end? We fall in and out of each other, in and out of God, with every breath, and with every holy action of our lovemaking. Our making love with one another becomes an exploration into the infinite. It is surrendering to the holiness of our God-bodies, and allowing the divine pleasure to be lived and expressed through us, in the most intimate and sacred way. Rumi writes,

> "At night we fall into each other with such grace ...
> ... Your eyes now drunk with God,
> mine with looking at you,
> one drunkard takes care of another" (32).

May we enter our lovemaking with the reverence and awe that God, and we, deserve. And may we allow its infinite nature to show itself to us, again and again and again.

Companion Meditation:
Come together with the intention of honoring the Holy of Holies within each person. Make an intentional space of sensuality through music, incense, candles, and anything else that will create for you "another world." Place aside all desires or need to possess. Rather come with reverence, knowing that in making love you are making God. You are creating the infinite love through your actions. Breathe together, caress each other, and let the Spirit take you into the Garden of Divine Delight.
(If alone, create a space as described above and come into your own Soul Garden. Invite the Spirit of God and let your spirits commingle).

Community Meditation:
We are in this world but not of the world. How does your community represent the Holy of Holies in the world? Joining together breathe into the depths of love, let any worldly feelings of jealousy, pride, insecurity, hatred, or other notions lie down. Breathe into the Holy Breath, and know you are something other. Know your community to be something other. Let that Holy Other fill your soul and the soul of your community with its unique spirit. Be a light unto the world.

35

Joyful Spirits

*I rejoice and exult with you in
the joy of the Spirit.*

—The Lady, 54

No one can give us our joy. No one can take away our joy. Joy is an inherent spiritual quality that we alone are responsible for, by finding it within. If we look for our joy in partnering with another, then we shall suffer disappointment again and again. Clare knew this path of disappointment well; and it began for her within a few days of her joining Francis and the brothers.

Clare held a vision of living and creating community with Francis and the brothers. She was so happy when she left her home to join them. Unfortunately, Francis had difficulty understanding what to do with his passionate love for Clare. Seemingly unable to live the "middle path" by combining his love for God with a physical expression of love for Clare, Francis embraced celibacy. Clare was subsequently confined within monastic walls. This was a great trial for her, as she longed to be with Francis, out serving the people and roaming in the woods, as she had previously done. Clare began to experience what it meant to live the life of surrender and non-attachment; she began the long journey of finding her own inner joy.

During one of their meetings, Clare and Francis were walking together in the snow. As Francis was preparing to leave, Clare asked when she would see him again. Francis replied, "When the roses will bloom in the spring." Clare caught her breath as she thought how long that would be, and then she looked ahead of her. There was a rosebush, and in that moment a rose came into full bloom. She knew at that instant that Francis was always with her, and even though they might not be together physically, their souls were joined. "What God has joined together, let not man separate" (Matt. 19:6).

Our own joining asks that we bring all of ourselves—physically, emotionally, and spiritually—to the grace of union. And it asks that when we come to lovemaking we come not seeking our joy but rather bringing the joy within us and offering it to our companions. In our love-making we offer ourselves to God and to each other; in this way we will enrich who we are, and who our companions are, and be given joy beyond our imaginings. It is here that we enter the true Temple of Love.

In the Gospel of Philip it is written, "In the Temple Space the form of union is different, although we employ the same name for it; but there exist forms of union higher than any that can be spoken, stronger than the greatest forces, with the power that is their destiny. Those who live this are no longer separated. They are one, beyond bodily distinction" (133). In this union we come to know the God-self residing within our souls and bodies, both our own and our companions. This recognition opens the way for true harmony and love to be lived. Again, the Gospel of Philip says, "Those who recognize each other know the joy of living together in this fullness" (133).

Clare was renowned for her joy. She walked a difficult path with Francis, but her spirit triumphed into its own love. She writes, "Truly I can rejoice and no one can rob me of such joy" (*The Lady*, 50). And, "Be very joyful and glad! Be filled with a remarkable happiness and a spiritual joy!" (*The Lady*, 45). For Clare and Francis, joy was present everywhere: within us, surrounding us, and even in situations that were difficult. We need to leap into the real joy that is ever present. A billboard message captures this imperative beautifully: "Misery has enough company. Dare to be happy!"

Companion Meditation:
Begin by coming deep within your own being, and ask for the spiritual joy
to become present to you. As you lie with your companion, let this joy spill
out from your soul and body, and give it as an offering to your partner.
Open your heart and soul, and allow yourself to receive your partners joy.
Let the Spirit lead you as you join your souls and bodies in the Union of
Joy.
(For those alone, ask that you may experience your innate joy and take the
time to deeply bask in this.)

Community Meditation:
How joyful is your community? Let this be a meditation of Joy. Come
together into the deep silence, and breathe into your spiritual joy. Let this
joy spill over into one another and the whole community. Know this to be
your true home. Commit to living this joy every day. Take this joy and
offer it to the world.

Fullness of the Senses: Mystical Union

*There is reverence for the divine
in the image of one another.*

—Ann Johnson

The maturity of mystical union is lived with the acknowledgment of each person's divine origin. It is also lived in a very practical and simple way through our earthly lives. The pathway of the mystical nature is essentially one of simplicity and love.

The *Fullness of the Senses* invites us to return to this simplicity through compassion, trust, conscious actions, and open and loving hearts. We are reminded to hold our dreams and visions lightly, not falling prey to a spiritual rigidity but allowing the spirit of love to renew us in every moment. To experience the fullness of our senses is to be in alignment with our physical, emotional, and spiritual selves, honoring the needs of each accordingly. When we come into this alignment we are taken into the world with new vision and new actions, and come to meet our many companions along the way.

36

Holiness of Love

*O sisters, see how brilliantly her feminine
sensibility shone.*

—The Lady, 137

Clare knew, and tasted deeply, her feminine nature. It was yet another
doorway into experiencing the richness and vastness of the eternal.
One aspect of the spiritual nature of a woman is the womb of compassion, that is, allowing for all beings to be held in the divine
embrace. It is written of Clare, "She, who soothingly refreshed our
hearts about the embrace of the divinity" (*The Lady*, 137).

Mother Mary was an important presence for Clare. As did the
Christ child, Clare climbed into Mary's arms and found solace and
strength in the divine Mother's nourishing love. Clare also had an
intimate connection with the Christ child himself, who spoke to her
and visually manifested in appearances that others heard and saw also
(*The Lady*, 179; *Peterson*, 301). Clare embodied these energies of both
mother and child within herself, compassionately embracing herself,
and those in need, and having the wisdom and simplicity of the child.

But Clare was also a passionate woman, continually pressing for
her ideal of the purity of heart, both within herself and within the
community. She showed enormous inner and outer strength and was
called a "new leader of women" (*The Lady*, 279). When a woman
truly enters into her divine womanly power, it is a great force, and it

can be intimidating for men. Yet the truth of this heavenly gift, that it is something to be shared to help ignite the divine masculine nature, makes it less threatening and more a holy invitation to enter into the truth of self.

It is well known that Francis had relations with only two women: the intimacy with Clare, and his "brotherly" affection with Jacopa. Clearly, he did not trust himself further. And what other beautiful feminine energies must he have missed out on through this mistrust. As we walk with our companions, if we are living with open hearts, other women and other men come before us all the time. Some make our hearts flutter with attraction, others take on a soul brother or sister relationship. In properly recognizing these companions, we need deep awareness of where our energy is being placed, and what is the truth of our intention.

For instance, if we find our attention being overly directed towards another, we can immediately bring our energy back to ourselves and breathe into the greater love. Sitting in the center of our loving being, we can allow all feelings of attraction to come and go, without the need to act on them, and without being pulled unconsciously into a situation that could cause emotional havoc, for ourselves, our companions, and the others concerned. When we are fully centered in our being, we can redirect our loving energy to our companions. Whenever our attention strays to another, a rift occurs with our companions. Whether we are aware of it or not, the relationship with them starts to fray. In directing our attention back to our companions, we bind the rift and open the door to even deeper relationship.

Unfortunately, when people begin to open their hearts to true intimacy, they can find difficulty in holding it lightly in the beautiful container of love. Either it becomes possessive and rigid or our energy inappropriately goes out to others. Or, of course, it can become too threatening, resulting in withdrawal. True love is for mature souls who can hold all things in their hearts, with an ever-awakening conscious awareness, and a commitment to become alert to any unconscious actions. Like Clare, we must be compassionate with ourselves and one another on our journey, and help one another come into that consciousness, or, the *holiness of love*. As Clare patiently walked with Francis, may we too offer our love and compassion to one another and remember these words of Clare: "The patience of those whose vision springs from a consideration of the Godhead produces the delights of paradise" (*The Lady*, 138).

Companion Meditation:
Come into the silence of your being. Bring the intention of being gentle with yourself. Breathe deeply into your own love and compassion, and sit here tenderly. When ready, remember a time when you felt an attraction for another person. Gently release and withdraw your energy from that person. Bless the person and send to him or her the greater love. Bless yourself, and sit in your own greater love. Continue with other attractions to other people as needed. When complete, send loving energy to your companion with the intention of healing any rift that has occurred between you, and open the way for even deeper communion. You may wish to seal this deeper joining with an external gesture, whether it be a kiss, a poem, or the commingling of energies and bodies. Let your soul decide.

Community Meditation:
Nothing destroys community more quickly than sexual attractions being unleashed and lived from non-integrity. Let this be a meditation to clear any sexual energy that has wounded or is wounding the community. Coming together in the spirit of love and forgiveness call upon the compassion of the Mother. Let all gently rest in silence in her arms. Let her loving tenderness soothe your soul. Allow any attractions to others to come and go, and bring yourself back to your own loving energy. Ask that you be blessed by God's compassionate love. Ask to be able to forgive those who have wounded you. Let your soul be healed. Let the community soul be healed. May you come together once more in love.

37

Spiritual Food

She greatly desired to eat with him ...
so sweetly, so sublimely ... the divine grace
descended upon them.

—De Robeck, 41

In the earliest Christian communities, the ritual of "breaking bread" was a simple meal shared in one another's homes. It served as a binding together of the community and a remembrance of Christ's message of the eternal love being here now, on earth, within each person. In coming together as a community and celebrating this truth, the early Christians were reminded that they were being spiritually and physically nourished by God, and by one another.

Clare often asked Francis to eat with her. For some reason he mostly denied this request. It was the brothers who persuaded Francis that he should do as she asked. He finally agreed, and he decided that they should eat in the woods near the Porziuncula Church, where Clare initially joined Francis and the brothers, and consecrated her life to God. Francis knew that Clare held this place deep in her heart, and he wanted her to be there again.

For this meal, Clare and Francis sat together. The other sisters and brothers sat around them. It is written "that the divine grace abundantly came upon them and all were lifted into an ecstatic and rapturous state" (De Robeck, 42). The Holy Spirit is known to be the energy of fire, and it is recorded that people from Assisi and the surrounding countryside saw a blaze burning brightly in the woods where Clare and Francis sat. Rushing to put out the flames, the villagers found instead a spiritual fire, burning in the hearts of Clare and Francis and the sisters and brothers present. All were ablaze with the fire of divine love in their souls, and all who saw them were blessed by this love (ibid.)

We today, with our overly rational minds, may scoff at this legend, but in contemporary Assisi the story is still told and believed. Those who have visited Assisi will know that extraordinary energies exist there and will find this story believable. We have to ask, is this why Clare requested so often to eat with Francis? Did she know the great power and spiritual mystery of breaking bread together? Was she attempting to reinstitute the meetings of the early Christians, where it was known that the Holy Spirit descended with fire? We cannot know. But it is clear that Clare's soul was aware of something of this spiritual mystery. She knew it was spiritual food that they were also eating.

To break bread together is a sacred act. But the sacredness has been hijacked by theologies and philosophies through the ages, and the ritual has lost its power and spiritual fertility. It is time to return to the simplicity of remembering, and the gift of sharing. That is, remembering who we are, and sharing who we are with others. In this way we naturally support one another from our being of love, and not from our doing of the mind and obligation. It is time to come together in openness, so that the divine grace can enflame our hearts with the radiant love. This is our gift to one another. This is the remembrance of Christ being lived.

Light and fire were commonly seen around the head and body of Clare (as also with Francis). A sister recorded, "It seemed, then, as if there were a great brilliance around holy mother Clare, not like anything material, but like the brilliance of stars. [And] after this ... another brilliance, not the color of the first, but all red in a way that seemed to emit certain sparks of fire" (*The Lady*, 179). When we truly open ourselves to the Light, it comes rushing in; even through the tiniest openings of our heart it will give itself to us. And the fire comes to burn away old pains and sorrows. We may feel the burning, emotionally and physically too. Though this may be difficult at times, it is a gift of liberation. It is freeing the heart to love in ways we do not even know are possible. May we be open to the spiritual food of divine grace and joyfully welcome whatever it brings.

Companion Meditation:
Let you and your companion come together with the conscious intention of entering into the sacred act of breaking bread. Jesus said, "Where two or more are gathered in my name, there I am also." Create a special meal or a simple dish. Enter into your own ritual, with personal prayers of thanksgiving and love. Bring a heart open to God and to the other. Let there be loving support for each other's spiritual journey. Open yourselves to be filled with the Divine Light, and let the Holy Fire of the Spirit descend upon you. You may want to make this a weekly ritual, or a time for special occasions.

Community Meditation:
Gather your community in silence, and let the intention be set for the sacred act of breaking bread. This may take the form of a special potluck dinner or a more ritualized form. Know that in entering into this ritual you are binding your community in love and divine grace, and that you come together to support one another on your spiritual journey. Let there be prayers of thanksgiving and a call for the Spirit to bless all your actions, now and in your daily life. Let this be a true communion of souls. You may want to make this a regular ritual, or for special occasions.

38

Soul Communion

*By the grace of God I have seen the
true face of Sister Clare.*

—De Robeck, 63

Francis showed great concern for Clare's spiritual journey here on earth. While returning from preaching in Siena, he was overcome with distress about her. Could her body and spirit withstand the great demands she was placing on herself? Was she pushing herself too hard to live the life she had chosen without consistent means of earthly support? Resting at a well and contemplating these troublesome thoughts, Francis looked down into the waters of the well. After a few moments he lifted his head, smiling. Turning to his traveling companion, Brother Leo, Francis said, "All my doubts have vanished. I have seen the true face of Sister Clare, and it is so pure and shining" (De Robeck, 63). In a place of soul communion, he saw the truth of Clare's spirit and was able to rest in peace through this vision.

Do we see the essence of our companions' spirit? What if we began our day, every day, with the intention of seeing our companions' spirit and essence? What if we began our day, every day, with the intention of seeing our own spirit and essence? Let us always begin with self first. For it is the eyes of our own spirit that will allow us to see the spirit of another. This is how Clare and Francis were able to truly see each other—they found the divine love living within their own selves and looked out with these radiant eyes of love at each other. To really see the soul of another is a great gift, to both the one being seen and the one seeing. Such communion allows for the divine essence of our being to grow stronger in daily living. It allows the ego to lie down more quickly and quietly. It opens the door for the true spirit to be lived on earth.

When our souls come into communion with each other, we have to be careful that we do not fall into enmeshment with our companions' lives. There must be room to breathe, and constant clarity about whether we are experiencing communion or identification. Communion allows two souls to be joined in the one love while simultaneously being fully embodied in their individual selves. Identification is a losing of self and a taking on of the traits and experiences of the other, or becoming overly concerned with their lives to the point of not fully experiencing your own life.

In 1225, Francis was inflicted by the stigmata, by which the wounds of Christ are literally manifested and experienced. At the exact time that Francis received the stigmata, Clare became dangerously ill, and her death was thought to be near. Clare harbored an inner fear that she would not survive if Francis died, and unconsciously or, perhaps, consciously was seeking her own death first. She did survive, however her soul was so strongly identified with Francis, who was now making his way towards Sister Death, that her body continued to respond with a dire illness. This passionate soul identification clearly was not healthy. Clare in fact experienced ill health for the remainder of her life. Was this an inability to move beyond her mourning over Francis's death? Or was God using her illness as purification for herself and others? Only God and the soul of Clare can answer that with the fullness of understanding.

As we come deeper into communion with one another, may we let the spirit of our selves guide us. May we release unhealthy identifications and see anew, every day, both ourselves and our companions.

Companion Meditation:
Come into the silence of your being, and breathe deeply here. Have the intention of opening to your inner divine love and essence. Sit quietly, allowing it to unfold. See where you may have unhealthy identifications with your companion. See how you may lose yourself when with him or her. Hold these places gently, and let them dissolve into the divine love. Commit to seeing and knowing your divine essence. Commit to seeing and knowing the divine essence of your companion.

Community Meditation:
Community life can quickly erode when confronted with many personalities. Let this be a meditation of the Return to the Essence. Come together with the intent of bringing your attention to the divine essence within each community member. Breathe deeply into the stillness of your being. Lay aside your small personality and those of your community. Let the greater self of love emerge within. Breathe deeply into this love. Feel that same divine love within everybody present. Honor and bless your essence. Honor and bless the essence of all around you.

39

Sacred Trust

*I entrust my soul and commend my
spirit to you.*

—The Lady, 130

Trust is imperative to any relationship. Without trust we withdraw
and hide, unable to stand in our nakedness. We become strangers to
one another, with loneliness and isolation as our companions. Trust
can be felt on a spirit level with another; there is a deep knowing that
this spiritual connection is bound in love. What takes time to develop
is trust on a psychological or soul level. Past wounds can clash and
create all sorts of false mistrust, further amplifying the original
wounds. This is sure death to love. What is required is a deep commitment to return again and again to our innate spirit, in order for
truth, clarity, and trust to be present on all levels.

Clare and Francis were bound by a sacred trust. They trusted each
other's inner spiritual life with God and were able to experience great
soul growth by opening to the wisdom of the other. They were equal
in love. Francis also trusted implicitly in Clare's healing abilities. He
sent people afflicted with mental disturbance, leprosy, and other ailments to her for healing. Clare was known to have cured many who
sought her help. She would say a prayer (so low that no one could
hear) and make the sign of the cross over the person in need, and he
or she would experience an instant and permanent cure. These heal-

ings continued after Clare's death, especially for those who traveled to her grave site (*The Lady*, 157–159).

Clare had complete trust in Christ, knowing that whatever she asked for would be given. This trust was the very basis of her life. She also knew that the cross of Christ was the sign of life, not of death. Making the sign of the cross reaffirmed for her that the resurrection of life is available to us here and now, and that the abundance of healing love is ever present. Clare also had a great reverence for the sacraments, in particular holy water and the Eucharist. They were for her external manifestations of the unseen Spirit, helping all to connect even more deeply with the divine body of love.

One of the most celebrated instances of Clare's unswerving trust was the threatened invasion of San Damiano by the Saracens (a marauding band of Muslim warriors). As they were scaling the walls, the sisters rushed to Clare in fear. Climbing from her bed, she prostrated herself on the floor in prayer and in love asked God to save the sisters, saying that she would be their ransom. Rising, she took the monstrance (which holds the Eucharistic body of Christ) and walked to the outer walls. The Saracens, upon seeing Clare, fled in fear. God did not need her sacrifice. Her complete trust saved the community. (Peterson, 235–236).

A year later, when Assisi was threatened by a large army, Clare's prayers were again requested. Gathering the sisters in the chapel, she placed ashes on their heads (an acknowledgment of total reliance on God) and ordered them to fast and pray. The next morning the attacking army was defeated. This deliverance is still celebrated in Assisi.

In our journeys with our companions, we must have the same trust in the power of our prayer. We do not pray for another to change; rather, we come with an open heart, asking that the Spirit will guide us ever more deeply into sacred communion, trusting in what is emerging from our union.

Companion Meditation:
Come into a place of stillness, and breathe deeply here. Let arise any feelings you have about trust. Do you trust yourself? Do you trust God? Do you trust your partner? Do not judge what arises; simply allow these feelings to emerge in your consciousness. Ask that whatever mistrust is present be dissolved. Let the Spirit guide you wherever it needs to take you.

Community Meditation:
Community cannot survive if members do not trust one another. So easily our trust can be violated. Let this be a meditation for the Renewal of Trust. Come prepared to allow the Spirit to heal all rifts. Breathe deeply into the stillness of your soul. Freely allow any feelings of mistrust to arise. Hand them over to the Spirit. Call on the healing power of Christ, and bless yourself and all of your community.

40

Physical Caresses

*But our flesh is not bronze nor is our
strength that of stone. I beg you, therefore,
dearly beloved, to refrain wisely ... from
an impossible austerity.*

—*Early Docs.,* 46

A common thread among the saints through the ages is their admonitions regarding caring for the physical body. The body suffered terribly at the hands of Christianity, particularly in the early Middle Ages. At this time human flesh came to be considered primarily as vulnerable to the temptations of greed and lust, which had to be mitigated at all cost. Fasting, flagellation, and avoidance of women were highly recommended. But the one we call the leader of Christianity, Jesus of Nazareth, sparingly entered into the first practice, did not touch the second, and had no problem enjoying the company of women.

Clare and Francis however, were born into an environment that held these accusatory beliefs about the body. Many saints spoke against austere practices, but somehow they would forget their own advice. Clare was known for fasting so excessive that it appears she did permanent damage to her health. She also wore clothing and slept on bedding that clearly gave her great discomfort. Only through Francis's firm and loving care did she relent in these practices. Others had tried to dissuade Clare from her over zealousness, but it was Francis to whom she listened.

Francis himself, early on after his conversion, practiced severe fasting and also damaged his health. Fortunately, he came to realize this as a mistake and would not allow others to repeat it. On his deathbed, he confessed that he had greatly erred against "Brother Body." In his childlike and literal interpretation of the Gospel, he also relinquished articles of clothing necessary for basic warmth and comfort, in particular his shoes. After receiving the stigmata, he was unable to walk barefoot, and even ordinary sandals failed to protect his wounded feet. Clare made him shoes out of soft kid leather with special padded soles that kept his wounds from coming into contact with the ground. She also wove cloth and made a liturgical robe for Francis, providing him with at least a change of clothes! Both these items, made from and with love, can be seen today in the reliquary chapel of the Basilica of Saint Clare.

In these examples we see the firm caress of Francis as he clearly pointed out Clare's mistaken devotion, and the gentle stroking of Clare's action as she provided the physical softness and warmth Francis needed. Both actions were appropriate; both were nonjudgmental. How often do we give to our companions with an air of judgment and superiority? Likewise in our communities, do we give out of honoring another's path, which may be a difficult one, or do we give out of obligation or pity?

May we gently caress, with love, our own bodies and those of one another in times of need, relinquishing judgment to the inherent love that lives so blessedly within us all.

Companion Meditation:
Sitting with your companion, come into the quiet of your being. Let your eyes gently close, and allow each breath to bring you into a steady calm. Let arise any places in your life where you may not feel supported. Do not blame anyone or fall into a victim mentality. Simply witness what arises. When you are ready open the eyes, allowing your partner whatever time

she or he needs. Let each then communicate to the other what has arisen.
Like Clare, listen, and see how you can support each other.
(If you are alone, see how your friends and family may support you).

Community Meditation:
How does your community support others, both within and outside the
community environment? Come together and let there be a gentle sinking
into group silence, allowing the Spirit to speak to the community body.
Feel the way that you, as part of this body, are called to honor the broken,
the wounded, and those who do not fit into society. Allow for the generosity of the Spirit to speak and act through you without the desire to "do
good" blinding your way. How can you support those in need without
judging them or enforcing any sense of their being victims?

41

Igniting Others

They live according to the form of the primitive
Church of which it is written:
"The multitude of believers was of one heart and one soul."

—*The Lady,* 428

Clare and Francis held firm to their own visions in creating community. They did not bow down before the ecclesiastical authorities or
change their visions in order to be accepted. Their firmness of heart
and mind did not make their lives easy. Francis was insulted and
harassed by Church and laity alike. Clare was constantly being told
how to live by bishops and cardinals. But these two inspired beings
listened only to the voice of God within, and to each other.

Clare taught that God calls us to great things. We are not to
diminish ourselves but to become the very love of Christ in this
world. We are to be mirrors and examples to others, that they may see
their own reflection in us. That is, that they may recognize their own
Christ within. Clare writes, "Recognize your vocation," abandon the
ways of the world and come into your "great joy" through the enlightenment of the Holy Spirit. We all have a vocation in this world. Clare
tells us to find and live this vocation with "eagerness and fervor of
mind and body," so that God may ever expand within us and rid the
world of the unhappiness that besets so many. (*The Lady,* 60–61).

In being the leader, the mother, of her community, Clare was adamant that she was to hold that position in love, gently and humbly guiding her sisters with the wisdom that God had given her. She was determined that no sister should be commanded to do anything that would go against her soul, and that no one would ask of another something she herself would not be willing to undertake. Leadership for Clare was to be based in love and lived in love, and she intended for the sisters to acknowledge her teachings out of love. Adherence was not to come from a hierarchical sense of obedience but rather be motivated by the recognition of love being offered for the expansion of their souls.

Clare succeeded in living as she desired. Her service to love spread far beyond the walls of San Damiano. Her radiating heart ignited laywomen and men, bishops, cardinals, and Popes. None could deny the strength and purity of the love living within her. Her very presence was sought as a beacon to the wandering hearts trying to find their way home. Cardinal Hugolino wrote of the sorrow he felt after leaving her presence, describing her as "that joy of heavenly treasure." He recognized the truth of her vocation and supported her vision and that of Francis. Even when he became Pope (as Gregory IX) some years later, he sought Clare's spiritual counsel and acknowledged how she was "walking and living in the truth of the Spirit ... and [how she] embraced the intimate love." He also wrote that she should forget the past, "as you have learned from us." (*The Lady*, 129–132). May we have more leaders in our churches who are humble enough to recognize the spirit of the living truth!

In sharing their inner God love with each other, Clare and Francis fell deeply into the wellspring of love. By falling so deeply into themselves and God, they both found their vocations, which were to take love, and live and share it with their communities. It was these communities that Jacques de Vitry was writing about in the quotation at the opening of this chapter, whereby they were living as "one heart and soul." This was the form that Clare and Francis lived together, even though they were so often physically apart. This was the form that they gave to the world. They became one heart and soul with God, with each other, with their communities, and beyond, to include all beings. It was their example of this living love that ignited many souls to join them. Living in a unified love is a dream of many in our world today. May we, like Clare and Francis, create it and make it so.

Companion Meditation:
Come and sit in the presence of love. Let your soul be immersed in this love. Ask what is your true vocation in this world. Allow the answer to unfold as it desires. You may only receive glimpses to begin with, or you may receive images of things that need to be accepted before your vocation can be revealed. Everything is preparing us for our work in the world. Be attentive to what you are given and commit to supporting yourself in what is required. Commit also to supporting your companion's vocation.

Community Meditation:
Do you support one another in your community to realize your vocations? Let this be a meditation of Vocational Support. Gathering in the presence of love, lay down your smaller thoughts of what you think you are here to do. Lay down also your thoughts of what you think others are here to do. Open to the spirit of love and let the truth of your life be revealed to you. Be open to seeing the gifts of others. Do not force or interfere. Let the Spirit reveal at will. Hold all gently in your heart, and let the Spirit guide your actions.

42

Lover's Dreams

Come, take and drink.

—Peterson, 186

Our minds and hearts are full of dreams and wishes, dreams for the future and wishes for love. And very often these dreams and wishes carry vestiges of our cultural conditioning, or act as means of escape from our past experiences. When we are opening the doorway for something authentically new to be created, we may have the clarity of vision, but are we ready for it? We must look at our dreams and measure them against our reality. We may simply need to lay our dreams down for a while and allow life to unfold in its own gentle way and time, bringing our souls into exactly the place they need to be.

Our night dreams can disclose to us the subconscious workings of our psyche, or as Peterson writes (185), they can "reveal the essential truth behind the apparent." The following dream of Clare gives us a clear indication of the depth of her union with the soul of Francis. She was climbing a very high stairway but quickly and with great ease. She was going to Francis, and when she reached him, he bared his breast and told her, "Come, take and drink." Clare sucked from his breast, and when she finished he told her to drink more. She did, and "what she had tasted was so sweet and delightful that she in no way could describe it." After she had finished drinking, the nipple of Francis remained between her lips. Upon taking it from her mouth, she saw that it was "gold and so clear and bright that everything was seen in it as in a mirror" (Peterson, 186).

One of the greatest gifts we can receive from our companions is spiritual nourishment. This is what Clare is receiving in her dream. She is symbolically being nourished by the breast, by the very heart of Francis, but in offering her the golden nipple, which acts as a mirror, he is giving her the ability to witness her own golden self with truth and clarity. This is the purity of mystical union—spiritually feeding another to come into her or his own love. Too often in our relationships we reflect only the smallness of the self, and we get lost there, forgetting that the golden self is the true reflection. The small self is simply psychological dross asking to be released. Do not look too long at these manifestations—they are arising to be let go of, not to be clung to.

We need to ask these questions: Am I being spiritually nourished through my companionship? Am I allowing myself to be spiritually nourished? Often our ideas of how that nourishment should take place hinder the nourishing from occurring. Our fears will convince us that we need certain perimeters for nourishment to occur, or our vision for how that nourishment should manifest may have overly strict guidelines. Certainly we must be wise and take care of ourselves, but we may also need to relax for a time our vision of a desired-for future, no matter how we came by it, and open to what truly stands before us. There can be great freedom and greater clarity in dealing with reality as it is. Know that the vision will reemerge when it is time.

Clare's journey was one of constant surrender of her vision and desires for a perceived life with Francis, yet their love continued to develop deep within their souls. We have so many companions here on earth, and so many different types of companionship. It is up to us to explore these with maturity and respect, and to discover the exact nature of each companionship. Is it a healing exchange, a brother or sister relationship, a companion for a time, or a companionship with deeper dimensions? Certainly our dreams and wishes will delude us at times, but if we are intimate and honest with ourselves, all will become clear in its own way and time. Most important is that we be gentle and loving with ourselves, and with the other. In this way, the golden self will emerge to reflect the truth of who we really are, and we will find our way into the lived dream of companionship with ease.

Companion Meditation:
Bring yourself into a place of gentle quiet. Ask, "Am I being spiritually nourished? Am I spiritually nourishing myself?" Allow any thoughts and feelings to arise around these questions without judgment. See how you may bring nourishment to your soul. Commit to following what you see. Feel how this commitment affects your companionship, in both giving and receiving nourishment. Explore the possibilities with your companion.

Community Meditation:
The basis of spiritual community is to provide nourishment to the souls of all members and the body of the community itself. Come together with the intention to renew spiritual nourishment for all. Breathe deeply into the spirit of your community, and ask for the refreshment of your souls. Let all visions, all goals, all desires fall into the hands of God. Ask that the golden self of you and your community be gently revealed.

Conclusion:

Falling into Love and Life

*The supreme happiness in life is the conviction
that we are loved.*

—Victor Hugo

Every being on this earth deserves to be happy. Every being deserves to be loved. Can you imagine our world with this happiness and love abounding? Keep imagining, keep seeing, and start living it, remembering the words of Clare as she was departing from this life: "Always be lovers of your souls and those of all your sisters." To find within ourselves the conviction that we are loved—what a blessing! To have that conviction confirmed by the people around us—what a beautifully quiet bliss.

As we take responsibility for finding our own love, we begin to understand that love is not something we do, it is who we are. We do not have to give our love to anybody. In our being who we are, the love merely flows as a gentle river, streaming from one heart to another. We do too much in our world, including trying to love. May we return to the tenderness of our innate nature and by simply being allow the true love to flow gently and naturally into, and out of, our being.

This pathway of love is not always an easy one. All the saints have known this. Clare writes:

"And because straight is the way and the path, and narrow is the gate through which one passes and enters to life, there are few who both walk it and enter through it. And if there are some who walk that way for a while, there are very few who persevere on it. But how blessed are those to whom it has been given to walk that way to persevere till the end" (*The Lady*, 64).

Yes, at times this journey is difficult, but it is becoming easier. We have many dedicated souls living on our earth who are opening the way for all to walk through the narrow gate. We are here to help and heal and love one another in varied ways. Paradoxically, then, we are responsible for all beings coming to know their happiness and their love. Let this knowledge spread in a healthy way.

In the passage just quoted, Clare writes that life is what we enter through the narrow gate. Love and life are synonymous. Anybody who falls into love immediately opens to life, and those who choose life, find love. A loving awareness of this sisterly and brotherly relationship between life and love can help us open our hearts, so that we can truly experience the glories of what it is to live on this earth.

May we take our bodies, with their delectable senses, and our souls, with their innate wisdom, and honor them as they deserve. May we enter into the depths of receptivity, and allow joy, and life, and love to once more live and reign within us.

Resources

Bibliography

Armstrong, Regis J. (edited and translated) *Clare of Assisi, Early Documents*, Paulist Press, New York, 1988.

Armstrong, Regis J. (edited and translated) *Clare of Assisi, The Lady, Early Documents,* New City Press, New York, 2006.

Camille, Michael. *The Medieval Art of Love,* Harry N. Abrams, Inc., Publishers, London, 1988.

Camus, Albert. *The Rebel: An Essay on Man and Revolt,* Vintage International, New York, 1991.

Johnson, Ann. *Miryam of Nazareth*, Ave Maria Press, Notre Dame, Indiana, 1984.

Johnson, Robert, and Ruhl, Jerry, M. *Balancing Heaven and Earth,* Harper Collins, San Francisco, 1998.

De Robeck, Nesta. *St. Clare of Assisi,* The Bruce Publishing Company, Milwaukee, 1951.

Ladinsky, Daniel. *I Heard God Laughing: Renderings of Hafiz*, Sufism Reoriented, 1996.

Ledoux, Claire Marie. *Clare of Assisi: Her Spirituality Revealed in Her Letters*, Translated by Colette Dees. St. Anthony Messenger Press, Cincinnati, Ohio, 1997.

Leloup, Jean-Yves. *The Gospel of Philip*, Translated by Joseph Rowe, Inner Traditions, Rochester, Vermont, 2003.

Leloup, Jean-Yves. *The Sacred Embrace of Jesus and Mary*, Translated by Joseph Rowe, Inner Traditions, Rochester, Vermont, 2006.

Merrill, Nan, C., *Psalms for Praying*, Continuum, New York, 2004.

Moyne, John, and Barks, Coleman. *Open Secret: Versions of Rumi*, Shambhala, Boston, 2000.

Parker, Hershel. *The Norton Anthology: Walt Whitman, Emily Dickinson*, WW. Norton & Co., New York, 1998 (Fifth Edition).

Peterson, O.S.F., Ingrid, J. *Clare of Assisi: A Biographical Study*, Franciscan Press, Quincy, Illinois, 1993.

Rilke, Rainer Maria. (Transl. by Leishman, J.B.) *Poems of Rainer Maria Rilke, Everyman's Library*, Random House, 1996.

Sabatier, Paul. *Life of St. Francis of Assisi*, Hodder & Stoughton, London, 1913.

Schaberg, J. *The Illegitimacy of Jesus*, Harper Collins, San Francisco, 1987.

Sister Frances Teresa OSC. *This Living Mirror, Reflections on Clare of Assisi*, Orbis Books, New York, 1995.

Tejpal, Tarun, K. *The Alchemy of Desire*, Ecco, New York, 2005.

Thomas of Celano. *The Life of Saint Clare*, Translated and Edited by Fr. Paschal Robinson, The Dolphin Press, 1910.

Permissions
Acknowledgments

Acknowledgments

I would like to thank the dear brothers of Little Portion Friary, Long Island, New York, who through the true Franciscan generosity, opened their home and hearts to me, feeding me in both body and soul, as I wrote a major portion of this book at their monastery. They also kindly gave me unlimited access to the archives of the Poor Clares, housed at Little Portion.

Thank you to the Lyman Fund for financially assisting me in visiting Assisi, Italy. And to Ruth and Bruce Davis who made my journey there both soulful and fun-filled.

Many thanks to my editor, Susan Brown, who brought my sometimes, wandering words into greater clarity.

And mostly, deep gratitude to the many companions I have met along the way. You have loved me and helped me to heal. You have brought me again and again into my own delicate place of resurrected love. I thank you.

About the Author

MEGAN DON was born in New Zealand and spent many years traveling to pursue her interests in spirituality and mysticism. Seeking the mystical element in Christianity she was led to spend time working and living with monastic orders, which included the Franciscans, the Carmelites, and the Cistercians.

Megan undertook her university studies in Comparative Religions and Psycho-Analytical Studies, and continues her studies in Leadership and Spirituality and Developing Spiritual Communities.

She is the author of *Falling Into the Arms of God: Meditations with Teresa of Avila*, which won the 2006 Ashton Wylie/New Zealand PEN Society of Authors Award in the "Mind, Body, Spirit" category for excellence in authorship. She is currently translating the poetry of Teresa of Avila.

Megan is a spiritual counselor and offers retreats on Christian mysticism, including the teachings of Teresa of Avila, Clare of Assisi, The Divine Mother, and how to practically live the mystical life in the world. She also takes pilgrimages to Assisi, Italy, where participants are immersed in the sacred ethos of Clare and Francis of Assisi.

Please see her website at www.mysticpeace.com
Email: clarepilgrimage@yahoo.com

978-0-595-47068-(
0-595-47068-8

Printed in the United States
207607BV00001B/13-63/P